AF269666

Boston's reputation makes me cringe. When I tell friends from my hometown of Chicago that Boston is America's most beautiful city, I'm always met with confusion. "Isn't it overrun with belligerent sports fans and college kids?" they ask me as they recall the tourist traps they visited during their stay. My beloved Boston is so misunderstood. To me, it's the closest one can get to Europe without flying overseas. It's an insanely clean, breathtakingly gorgeous place where cobblestone streets, gas-lit lamps, and intricate brownstone homes are the norm. It's a place where everything is charming and historic, right down to our teensy little ballpark that dates back to 1912.

Yes, we have some rowdy sports fans, some college kids and some lovable Boston attitudes: horn-beeping, smack-talking folks with beers in their hands and no "filtahs" on their mouths. But quintessential Bostonian traits aside, people here are incredibly multicultural and their diversity is reflected in the city's many magical little shops and restaurants.

the hunt boston writer

brittany fischer

Brittany Fischer has been known to jump straight into a cab at the mere mention of an extraordinary meal, cocktail or shop. When asked what she majored in at Boston University, she deadpans, "Restaurants, coffee shops, bars and boutiques." In addition to becoming a Boston aficionado, Brittany was actually studying journalism and her writing has since graced the pages of Boston's most popular newspapers and magazines, as well as her blog, sheiswhosheis.com. In the rare event that she is not eating, caffeinating, drinking, shopping or writing, she's on a long walk, wearing headphones and extremely impractical shoes, scouting out new places to go.

Where to Lay your Weary Head   5

BACK BAY   10–21
Ball and Buck   12
Bodega   13
Casa Romero   14
Deuxave   15
Island Creek Oyster Bar   16
Jillian's   17
Lolita Cocina & Tequila Bar   18
The Corner Tavern   19
Trident Booksellers & Café   20
Yawkey Way Store   21

Brewed Awakening   22

BEACON HILL   24–33
Beacon Hill Bistro   26
Crush Boutique   27
Cynthia Driscoll Interiors   28
December Thieves   29
Grotto   30
Holiday   31
The Paramount   32
The Tip Tap Room   33

Architectural Gems   34

NORTH END   36–45
Carmen Trattoria   38
Giacomo's Ristorante   39
L'Osteria   40
Mike's Pastry vs Modern Pastry   41
Pizzeria Regina   42
Salumeria Italiana   43
Shake the Tree   44
Stanza dei Sigari   45

Food Trucks   46

WATERFRONT AND DOWNTOWN 48–55

Café Fleuri	50
JM Curley	51
Nebo Cucina & Enoteca	52
O Ya	53
Quincy Market	54
Tia's	55

SOUTH END 56–69

Blackbird Doughnuts	58
Bobby from Boston	59
Follain	60
Hudson	61
Myers and Chang	62
Niche	63
Olives & Grace	64
South End Buttery	65
SoWa Vintage Market	66
Stella	67
Stir	68
Vejigantes	69

Game On **70**

SOUTH BOSTON AND SEAPORT 72–83

75 on Liberty Wharf	74
American Provisions	75
Blue Dragon	76
KO Pies	77
Lincoln Tavern & Restaurant	78
Local 149	79
Mul's Diner	80
Neatly Nested Design & Decor	81
Stephi's in Southie	82
The Daily Catch	83

Hotspots for New England Fare **84**

CHARLESTOWN SOMERVILLE   86–95

Highland Kitchen   88
Magpie   89
Pier 6   90
Sound Bites   91
Tangierino Chophouse and Tapas   92
The Boston Shaker   93
The Neighborhood Restaurant & Bakery   94
The Warren Tavern   95

Boston After Dark
Laugh It Off   96
Cocktail Bars   99

CAMBRIDGE   102–113

Alden & Harlow   104
Bondir   105
Follow the Honey   106
Forty Winks   107
Grolier Poetry Book Shop   108
Hungry Mother   109
Life Alive   110
Mr. Bartley's Gourmet Burgers   111
Sofra Bakery   112
The Tannery   113

ALLSTON BROOKLINE, JAMAICA PLAIN   114–125

Busy Bee Restaurant   116
Clear Flour Bread   117
Coolidge Corner Theater   118
Lone Star and Deep Ellum   119
Mint Julep   120
Oishii Sushi Bar   121
Salmagundi   122
Ten Tables   123
Tres Gatos   124
Zaftig's Delicatessen   125
Walk This Way   126

THE BEACON HILL HOTEL & BISTRO

Classic townhouse hospitality

25 Charles Street (at Chestnut Street) / +1 617 723 7575 / beaconhillhotel.com

Double from $219

In the Lilliputian jewel that is Boston's historic Beacon Hill Hotel & Bistro, guests choose from 12 individually decorated guest rooms in two renovated 19th-century townhouses. There are two reasons aside from the accommodations to stay in this intimate gem: one, the location is unbeatable, and two, so is the food. In the warmer months, be sure to take advantage of the complimentary Picnic in the Park service: call the hotel's award-winning bistro an hour ahead to get your lunch or dinner packed in a picnic basket along with a blanket, and enjoy eating al fresco in the nearby picturesque Boston Public Garden (see pg 128).

THE COLONNADE

The ultimate urban oasis

120 Huntington Avenue (between Garrison and West Newton)
+1 617 424 7000 / colonnadehotel.com

Double from $199

Water babies, rejoice! Boston's outdoor pool selection is seriously dismal, but The Colonnade's rooftop piscine is a glorious social scene with private cabanas, sweeping skyline views, handcrafted cocktails and summery eats like swordfish tacos. The cost of admission? An abysmal $40 per guest per day, but for hotel guests: free! Be warned, though: the tropical vibes here have been known to cause amnesia, a condition only exacerbated by the sleek, modern and spacious rooms. Repeat after me: I am in Boston, I am in Boston, I am in Boston.

THE ELIOT HOTEL

Boutique chic in Back Bay

370 Commonwealth Avenue (at Massachusetts Avenue)
+1 617 267 1607 / eliothotel.com

Double from $395

Just steps from Newbury Street, Boston's most popular shopping stretch, The Eliot Hotel is perfect for a bona fide fashionista. After a strenuous spending spree, you can rest your feet (but not wallet) in your designer-clad room, where you'll be happy to discover décor as chic as your new purchases. When you're ready for dinner, you can head downstairs to the dazzling contemporary French restaurant Clio, or sample some of Boston's finest sushi at the upbeat sashimi and sake bar, Uni.

THE ELIOT HOTEL
370

THE LENOX

A rest stop for legends

61 Exeter Street (at Boylston Street)
+ 1 617 536 5300 / lenoxhotel.com

Double from $370

Built by a guy whose "bros" were Winston Churchill and the Duke of Windsor, The Lenox has been a Boston landmark ever since its arrival in the heart of Back Bay in 1900. *The Boston Post* immediately tagged it "The Waldorf-Astoria of Boston." Babe Ruth hung out here, Judy Garland lived here, Duke Ellington composed here. As such, when I make a reservation, I feel that I'm making history. But even if it were brand spanking new, I'd still adore it. It's luxurious but unpretentious with a sophisticated European flair and a stylish cocktail bar. Above all else, it masterfully delivers that personal touch.

THE LIBERTY HOTEL

A palatial prison that isn't ironic

215 Charles Street (between Fruit and Cambridge)
+1 617 224 4000 / libertyhotel.com

Double from $229

You wouldn't want to spend a night in prison, right? Wrong. Since the Charles Street Jail of 1851 underwent its $150 million renovation, it has become a hotel that is also Boston's most (in)famous landmark on the nightlife circuit. Upon check in, you're handed a glass of Champagne. Come 9pm, you'll see the lobby transform into a glamorous soirée. Here, two restaurants and four of Boston's sultriest bars are linked by historic catwalks, which become actual fashion runways on Thursday nights. Because it's a party-going hotspot, locals frequently stay overnight here – the convenience of a bed only a few feet away is nearly as indulgent as the rooms themselves, which feature floor-to-ceiling windows with majestic skyline views. Families, keep out. Singles, welcome.

back bay

It's hard to believe that Boston's iconic Back Bay was a literal bay prior to a massive 19th-century filling project that transformed what once was water into buildable land. Striking and pristine, this residential neighborhood of beautifully preserved Victorian brownstones – the largest in the nation, I might add – seems more like a museum of the historic townhouses. I can attest to the fact that people truly do live here, because I did (in a teensy studio, but nonetheless), on the tucked-away stunner that is Marlborough Street, one block up from the Commonwealth Avenue Mall (which itself is a few steps away from the shopping hub of Newbury Street). You'd think I would've gotten used to the view, but I was always awed by the area's magnificent elegance, and I'd find myself wondering, 'What was Boston like before Back Bay?' The answer is: a very sad place indeed. You'll agree as you explore the quintessentially Bostonian showpiece, home to Newbury Street shopping.

1 Ball and Buck
2 Bodega
3 Casa Romero
4 Deuxave
5 Island Creek Oyster Bar (off map)
6 Jillian's (off map)
7 Lolita Cocina & Tequila Bar
8 The Corner Tavern
9 Trident Booksellers & Café
10 Yawkey Way Store (off map)

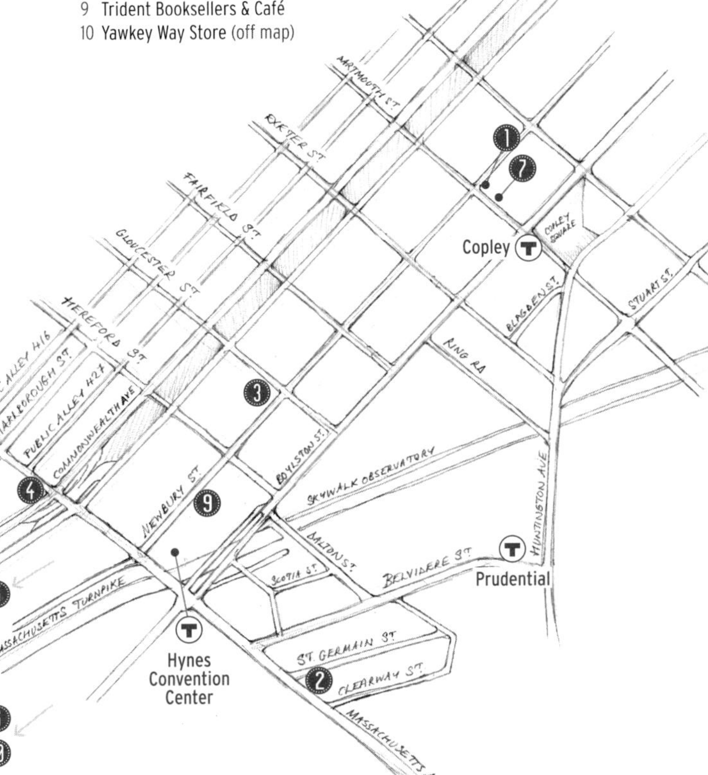

BALL AND BUCK

The perfect shop for urban lumberjacks

144B Newbury Street (at Dartmouth Street) / +1 617 262 1776
ballandbuck.com / Open daily

On my first visit here, I was seeking out a pine incense that a friend had recommended. When I walked in, though, I immediately noticed the hunting-inspired menswear: wonderfully masculine, high quality and different than what one usually finds on posh Newbury. This all-American company has "red, white and blue running through its veins," an associate told me as I fawned over the handsome flannel shirts that will populate the closet of my future husband. "We also have the best barbershop in town," he added, nodding toward the back, where a man was getting a hot towel shave while sitting in a '20s porcelain and chrome barber chair. His grin confirmed that this must be man heaven.

BODEGA

Secret sneaker and sportswear shop

6 Clearway Street (between Massachusetts and Dalton)
+1 617 421 1550 / shop.bdgastore.com / Open daily

From the sidewalk, Bodega's windows are crammed with toilet paper and generic bleach. It truly looks like the shadiest, most run-down convenience store in existence. Walk inside and it's a hodgepodge of dusty perishables and walls covered in stickers and marker inscriptions. Before you curse my name for directing you here, head to the archaic Snapple vending machine and find the broken tile on the floor in front of it. Step on that tile and voilà! The vending machine, which is actually a sliding door, opens to reveal an Aladdin's cave of sportswear. Gleaming mahogany shelves house Boston's freshest selection of graphic tees, hoodies, caps and old-school kicks: the sneakerhead's dream realized.

CASA ROMERO

The heart of Mexico in the heart of Back Bay

30 Gloucester Street (between Commonwealth and Newbury)
+1 617 536 4341 / casaromero.com / Open daily

It's possible that I have a penchant for hidden gems that are literally hidden underground. Buried in a dark alley, Casa Romero is particularly tough to uncover, but its Talavera-tiled door leads you down a set of stairs and straight into Mexico. Here, find my favorite outdoor patio (sunken and swathed in string lights) and margarita (cucumber, rimmed with Tajín). While your waiter will tell you everything is "nice" in his most adorable broken English, here's what you need to know: I found the ceviche just okay, but the sweet and smokey mole sauce made with over 20 ingredients, including chocolate and chili peppers, is utterly swoon-worthy. It has a cult following for a reason.

DEUXAVE

Contemporary French decadence

371 Commonwealth Avenue (at Massachusetts Avenue)
+1 617 517 5915 / deuxave.com / Open daily

As a creature of deviation, I rarely enjoy a dish so much that I order it
every time I return to the restaurant. That said, I will be forever faithful
to Deuxave's spiced Long Island duck breast, named one of Boston's
most memorable meals by *The Boston Globe*. As the tender medallions
with prune port gastrique melt in my mouth, and my expertly crafted
Kir Royale is illuminated by the twinkling tea lights, I cannot help but
channel Meryl Streep as Julia Childs, who, bewildered by each bite of
a sensationally good baguette, exclaims, "I feel that I am French...
I simply must be!" Me too, Ms. Childs. Me too.

ISLAND CREEK OYSTER BAR

Fish and bubbles for the seafarer

500 Commonwealth Avenue (at Raleigh Street) / +1 617 532 5300
islandcreekoysterbar.com / Open daily

Fittingly, the interior of Island Creek Oyster Bar shimmers like an iridescent oyster shell, thanks to the glittering silver décor. Despite the glossy surrounds and the fact that the seasonally influenced ocean catch is of the highest quality, you can just as easily swing by in your fan gear before catching a game at nearby Fenway Park as you can after you've dolled yourself up to make this your destination for the evening. With an extensive selection of shellfish (some of which are farmed by the co-owner himself), its prized crispy whole black bass and one of the city's best traditional lobster rolls (see pg 84), this is undoubtedly up there for the most scrumptious seafood in Boston.

JILLIAN'S

Boston's adult amusement park

145 Ipswich Street (at Lansdowne Street) / +1 617 437 0300
jilliansboston.com / Open daily

When it comes to bowling, all I have to say is: spare me (pun intended). Gutter balls are my speciality, but I once famously released my ball on my backswing and threw the ball into the seating area, putting many horrified onlookers in grave danger. The general public and I have since decided that I'm better suited to referee, which allows me to judge not only the game, but the food, drink and ambiance of the establishment as well. Jillian's is awesome because it's not just bowling (great news for me): it's a retro three-floor entertainment wonderland that also features tons of pool and foosball tables, two full-service restaurants and a wild nightclub. I certainly wouldn't call it sophisticated, but it's a trusty solution when I'm in search of a little something for everyone.

LOLITA COCINA & TEQUILA BAR

Literature come to life

271 Dartmouth Street (between Newbury and Boylston)
+1 617 369 5609 / lolitatequilabars.com / Open daily

The English Literature major in me can't help but find parallels between this swanky spot and Nabokov's novel. Submerged below the sidewalk, it feels a bit like a gothic dungeon: eerie, but in an oddly enticing way that's distinctly Humbert-esque. The extensive menu boasts over 180 tequilas, making it almost as lengthy as the book (but a much less anxious read). The feeling I have as I devour the innovative Mexican-inspired fare – particularly the Vertical Nachos, which features warm, thick chips standing in layers of beans, cheese, smoked bacon and guacamole, and the tomatillo coconut broth steamed mussels served with a grilled baguette and topped with cilantro – and two too many Broken Hearted Margaritas is the exact same one I had reading the book: undeniably guilt-ridden, but satisfied.

THE CORNER TAVERN

Wondrous wood-lined warmth

421 Marlborough Street (at Massachusetts Avenue)
+1 617 262 5555 / thecornerboston.com / Open daily

I am torn as to whether or not I should bring this upscale neighborhood pub to light, because it's my little secret and I'm very selective about who I let in on it. I have a good feeling about you though, so here it is: the pours are heavy, the food is divine – I have to call attention to the tortilla soup, and the proscuitto and mozzarella salad drizzled with basil dressing which, when available, are musts – and there's a jukebox. Never dead but rarely crowded, it's my first choice for two occasions: a solo weeknight dinner or a late night drunken dance party where nobody seems to care that I take full control of the tunes ('90s pop, baby – see you there!).

TRIDENT BOOKSELLERS & CAFÉ

Independent bookshop and full-service restaurant

338 Newbury Street (between Massachusetts and Hereford)
+1 617 267 8688 / tridentbookscafe.com / Open daily

I have been known to have breakfast here, stay through lunch, dinner
and a few glasses of wine, and close the place out at midnight. The wait
staff never flinch when I unload my laptop along with a mammoth tangle
of chargers (my life is one of wires) and a towering stack of notepads.
More likely, they'd balk if I didn't. The food is satisfactory, particularly the
in-house corned beef hash, and while it's a fine café, it's an exceptional
workspace. If you're in town on business, you can camp out here to hit
your to-do list with the help of anything from a shot of wheatgrass to an
espresso. When your brain is fried, browse the quirky collection of books
and magazines across two floors for inspiration.

YAWKEY WAY STORE

Because "Boston Strong" is a way of life

19 Yawkey Way (at Ralph's Way) / +1 800 336 9299
yawkeywaystore.com / Open daily

To be honest, sports aren't my thing. I've been known to channel
Derek Zoolander as I stare vapidly at the television, swooning over
Tom Brady and periodically asking, "Who's winning the match?"
That said, my camouflage Red Sox hat is a staple in my wardrobe.
Sometimes I even pair it with heels. To me, it's a sartorial reminder of
how much heart this city has. In the wake of the marathon bombing in
2013, Boston has displayed the most awe-inspiring, unshakable spirit.
Whether you're looking to rep the Red Sox or just want show support
for one of the strongest cities out there, Yawkey Way Store has the
largest selection of Boston-themed hats and apparel in town.

brewed awakening

Where to get your caffeine fix

RENDER COFFEE

Boston is home to over 100 colleges and universities and the city is brimming with so many wide-eyed, college-aged youths, that I often find myself wistfully murmuring, "Ah, to be a carefree student again." With the students comes their need to study, so the demands for free Wi-Fi and a constant flow of caffeine are high. Accordingly, our coffee shop game is very strong indeed.

Sip Café is a great urban oasis: a tiny glass structure that sits smack in the center of the chaotic Financial District, but somehow still manages to feel like a magical little tree house. Its pièce de résistance: the ginger latte.

On the completely opposite end of the spectrum, **Java House**, in Southie, is where it's at if you like iced coffee with a side of Boston accent and the attitude to match. But this place isn't the kind of coffee shop where you set up camp for the entire day – it's standing room only and serves as a quick pit stop for its many local regulars, but makes up for its lack of aesthetics in "flavah." The selection ranges from pistachio to blueberry cheesecake to thin mint. Their most popular pick is snickerdoodle, or "snicks" as they say around here.

EQUAL EXCHANGE CAFÉ
226 Causeway Street (between North Washington and
Beverly), +1 617 372 8777, equalexchange.coop
open daily

JAVA HOUSE
541 East Broadway (between G and H)
+1 617 268 3117, facebook.com/Java-House, open daily

RENDER COFFEE
563 Columbus Avenue (between Massachusetts and
Wellington), +1 617 262 4142
rendercoffeebar.com, open daily

SIP CAFÉ
0 Post Office Square (at Franklin Street)
+1 617 338 3080, sipboston.com
closed Saturday and Sunday

THINKING CUP
85 Newbury Street (between Clarendon and Berkeley)
+1 617 247 3333, thinkingcup.com, open daily

When I know I have a stressful day ahead, I head to **Render Coffee** in South End. If the cozy yet airy, hipster yet unpretentious atmosphere doesn't give you a positive perspective, the masterful pour-over java surely will.

Over in North End, If you're looking to scoop up some good karma with a cup of fair trade coffee, try **Equal Exchange Café**. Randomly enough, you'll also find the best spring rolls in the city here. Careful though, they often sell out before noon.

Finally, **Thinking Cup** and I have been through a lot. When I first laid eyes on its dramatic crystal chandeliers, it was love at first sight. Then I discovered there's no Wi-Fi and my heart shattered. Now, I love it for exactly what it is: a glamorous, social approach (in the old school, non-Facebook sense) to coffee, and a destination in and of itself on Newbury Street.

beacon hill

The excruciatingly charming Beacon Hill is the highest point in central Boston, and one of our oldest communities. Its earliest residents began their mornings by pouring the contents of their chamber pots out their doors, creating a stream that rushed down the south slope as if it knew it had no place in the city's most desirable neighborhood. Thankfully that no longer happens, but architecturally, the area remains virtually untouched with every restaurant, every shop so small and quaint you might start to feel like Gulliver in a world better suited for Thumbelina. As you wander the cobblestone streets shaded by bountiful flowering trees and bustling with trendsetting parents out for a walk with their children and designer dogs, look out for the following highlights – they're easy to miss.

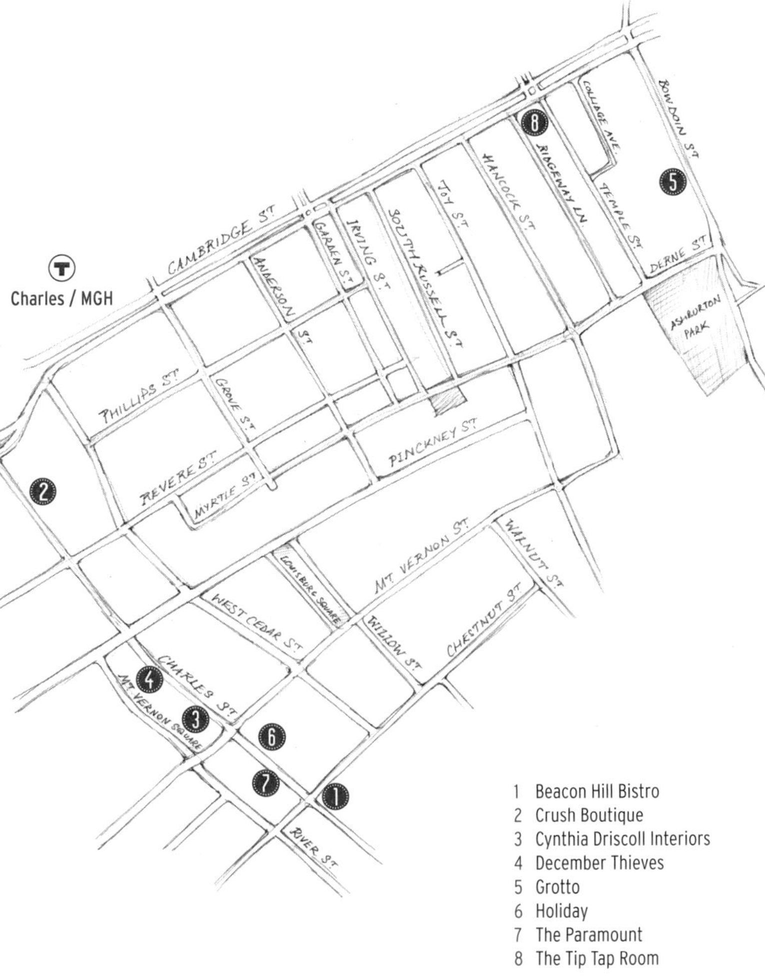

1 Beacon Hill Bistro
2 Crush Boutique
3 Cynthia Driscoll Interiors
4 December Thieves
5 Grotto
6 Holiday
7 The Paramount
8 The Tip Tap Room

BEACON HILL BISTRO

Comfort to defeat the winter blues

25 Charles Street (at Chestnut Street) / +1 617 723 7575
beaconhillhotel.com/the-bistro / Open daily

By around March every year, when Bostonians are sick of snow and craving spring, the city descends into madness. Personally, the temporary insanity manifests itself in drastic changes to my hair, be it a bad dye job or cut. I'm learning to fight these urges, though, and Beacon Hill Bistro has become my cure-all for when they become nearly unbearable. The eponymous bistro of Beacon Hill Hotel & Bistro (see pg 5) features two roaring fireplaces and a decadent French menu. The roasted chicken breast with duck fat truffle vinaigrette is extraordinarily juicy, and the devil's food cake with salted caramel ice cream is no-bite-left-behind delicious. BHB's power is so substantial that in the height of winter I actually find myself content to endure yet another snowstorm, my yearnings for warmer weather cast aside.

CRUSH BOUTIQUE

The friendliest shop in Boston

131 Charles Street (between Silver Place and Revere)
+1 617 720 0010 / shopcrushboutique.com / Open daily

Crush Boutique feels less like a store, and more like the closet of your best-dressed girlfriend. You know, the one whose eyes light up when you timidly mention that you're not sure what to wear to an upcoming date/interview/event, who then grabs your hand and yanks you toward her wardrobe? Yeah, I actually don't have a friend like that either, and until I do, this boutique is my saving grace. Owners Rebecca and Laura are childhood friends and their undyingly honest assistance makes it seem as though they're my lifelong friends too – when playing dress up with them, I feel like Tai getting a makeover from Cher and Dionne in a real life version of *Clueless*.

CYNTHIA DRISCOLL INTERIORS

Imaginative pieces for the home

70 Charles Street (between Mount Vernon and Pinckney)
+1 617 367 6770 / cynthiadriscollinteriors.com / Open daily

I want my home to be a wonderland of interesting and beautiful treasures, a place where, in every room, my house guests will marvel over my many whimsical pieces and wonder where I've found them. Paris, Dar es Salaam, Bangkok, I'll reply as they widen their eyes, impressed by my cultured ways. Until I can afford to travel the world to shop for home goods, the honest answer will be Cynthia Driscoll Interiors. An acclaimed Boston designer, Driscoll opened this showroom to display her distinct style to prospective clients while filling the consumer need for unique home ornamentation, much to the delight of wannabes like me.

DECEMBER THIEVES

Cool girl threads

88 Charles Street (between Pinckney and Mount Vernon)
+1 617 982 6802 / decemberthieves.com / Open daily

Ah, the ever elusive cool girl. She saunters to her closet, randomly plucks out a few garments, grabs some jewelry and piles it all on. The whole process takes about five minutes and in the end she looks miraculous. I've tried it and instead ended up looking like a rambunctious preschooler who had spent too long playing dress up unsupervised. Jewelry designer Lana Barakat, however, is actually one of those cool girls, and her shop is a quirky array of unique pieces found on her worldly travels, be it a chic wine bottle stop, a scarf that can turn any outfit into a "look" or a cocktail ring that elicits compliments from all who see it.

GROTTO

Underground Italian decadence

37 Bowdoin Street (between Derne and Cambridge)
+1 617 227 3434 / grottorestaurant.com / Open daily

Tucked below Bowdoin Street in the shadow of the Massachusetts State House, Grotto is a cozily candlelit subterranean hideaway with an inconspicuous exterior, but don't let that deter you. As you pull aside the velvet curtain in the entryway, you'll find the flickering cave buzzing with savvy Yelp-surfers and knowing neighbors. Sure, the deep red décor is a bit shabby and the fake flowers a bit dusty, but somehow this adds to its romance. Just how romantic is it, you ask? While dining there with an engaged female friend, the short rib gnocchi with gorgonzola melting in our mouths, the wine bringing a flush to our cheeks, we found ourselves starry-eyed and giggling like spellbound honeymooners.

HOLIDAY

Lesser-known labels and reworked vintage

53 Charles Street (between Mount Vernon and Chestnut)
+1 617 973 9730 / holidayboutique.net / Open daily

"Welcome to the Dollhouse," reads the sign on the doors of this tiny boutique. Indeed, once inside I feel like a doll, changing from one stylish masterpiece to another. Showcasing smaller fashion houses from the U.S., this store offers me what I can't find elsewhere. For those in fear of showing up in the same dress as another girl, leave your worries at the door. What truly makes Holiday special, though, is their Pretty Little Vintage line, where the boutique owners transform second-hand pieces. By the time they hit the racks, they're reimagined and renewed, but without the price tag to match.

THE PARAMOUNT

Friendly neighborhood eatery since 1937

44 Charles Street (between Mount Vernon and Chestnut)
+1 617 720 1152 / paramountboston.com / Open daily

Let me tell you a story about The Paramount. A friend of mine had just adopted the world's sweetest kitten and was ravenous but couldn't bear to part ways with his brand new ball of fluff. So he brought her here for a hearty brunch. He sat her in the chair opposite his and gave her a portion of his entrée, which she ate standing on her hind legs with her front paws resting on the table. This scene, I hope, demonstrates how welcoming the staff is, and how down-to-earth the surroundings and clientele are. The food, like the atmosphere, is casual, comforting perfection. Whether you're beginning the day with caramel and banana French toast, or ending it with sizzling steak frites and a glass of Chianti, there are no wrong moves here.

THE TIP TAP ROOM

Wild game and craft beer

138 Cambridge Street (between Ridgeway Lane and Temple)
+1 857 350 3344 / thetiptaproom.com / Open daily

At The Tip Tap Room one can choose from over 36 beers on tap to pair with a variety of imaginative and exotic tips. Steak is a given, but Chef Brian Poe blows the basics out of the water with options like elk, antelope, swordfish, rabbit, buffalo and yak. If I were to dream up a place where the ultimate man's man would most enjoy his brewski and beef, I'd envision some kind of supreme man cave of a garage, so the fact that the dining room has giant retractable firehouse-style doors that open up to Cambridge Street is extremely appropriate. I know I said Ball and Buck (see pg 12) in Back Bay was man heaven, but now I think this might be it.

architectural gems

Because your eyes should feast, too

If NYC is the city that never sleeps, Boston is the city that sleeps a lot. The whole town shuts down by 2am, a point of contention for night owls like me. But what it lacks in terms of nightlife, it compensates for with its stupendously beautiful architecture. After you've seen the obvious beauties (the glittering gold dome of the The Massachusetts State House, and the paradoxical mirroring of Trinity Church in the modern John Hancock Tower), try these lesser-known showpieces.

Every home in Back Bay is a stunning 19th-century work of art, but **The Burrage House** stands out, even amongst its striking neighbors. The impossibly intricate stonework features 30 cherubs, 50 gargoyles and 300 bibliophiles. Truly fit for royalty, it's all too appropriate that it was once home to the king of Boston, New England Patriots quarterback Tom Brady.

The urge to peek inside one of these anything-but-humble abodes may become unbearable, but thanks to the **Gibson House Museum** it is entirely satiable. Untouched since 1860, this unspoiled single-family residence serves as a time capsule of domestic life for a well-to-do Boston family. Can't get enough? Beacon Hill's **Nichols House Museum**, a four-story townhouse from 1804, is another Victorian highlight.

GIBSON HOUSE MUSEUM
137 Beacon Street (between Arlington and Berkeley)
+1 617 267 6338, thegibsonhouse.org
open Wednesday–Sunday

NICHOLS HOUSE MUSEUM
55 Mount Vernon Street (at Walnut Street)
+1 617 227 6993, nicholshousemuseum.org
closed Sunday and Monday

RH BOSTON, THE GALLERY AT THE HISTORIC
MUSEUM OF NATURAL HISTORY
234 Berkeley Street (between Newbury and Boylston)
+1 857 239 7202, restorationhardware.com, open daily

THE BURRAGE HOUSE
314 Commonwealth Avenue (at Hereford Street)

THE CHRISTIAN SCIENCE PLAZA
210 Massachusetts Avenue (between Huntington and
Belvidere), +1 617 450 2000, christianscience.com
open daily

If you've ever lost track of time wandering around a fancy-pants furnishings store, schedule at least an hour for **RH Boston, The Gallery at the Historic Museum of Natural History**. Reminiscent of the palace of Versailles, it's a paradise of trickling fountains, sparkling chandeliers, dramatic mirrored archways, boasting a 24-foot illuminated steel Eiffel Tower and an 1892 traction-and-counterweight elevator replica.

Finally, I sometimes suspect that **The Christian Science Plaza** was designed purely for my own romantic ice cream consumption on dewy summer nights. The 670-foot long reflection pool lights up as the sun goes down, and the public fountains (open until 9pm) provide me with the pleasant soundtrack of children laughing in the distance. The nearby gardens lend a sweet aroma to the air, and the massive, dramatic church never fails to take my breath away.

north end

North End, Boston's Little Italy, is only one square mile but has the most flavor in the entire city – and I mean that literally. With more than 60 restaurants, the neighborhood is filled with the wafting aromas of fresh basil, garlic and tomato sauce. Of course, it is also rich with Italian culture and a colorful cast of characters. Here, you'll find trios of shirtless old men plopped into beach chairs in the middle of the sidewalk, smoking cigars without an ounce of concern for the tourists trying to squeeze by and women jutting their heads from windows, shouting in Italian. Thus, be it your craving for pasta or people watching, North End won't disappoint.

1 Carmen Trattoria
2 Giacomo's Ristorante
3 L'Osteria
4 Mike's Pastry (A) vs Modern Pastry (B)

5 Pizzeria Regina
6 Salumeria Italiana
7 Shake the Tree
8 Stanza dei Sigari

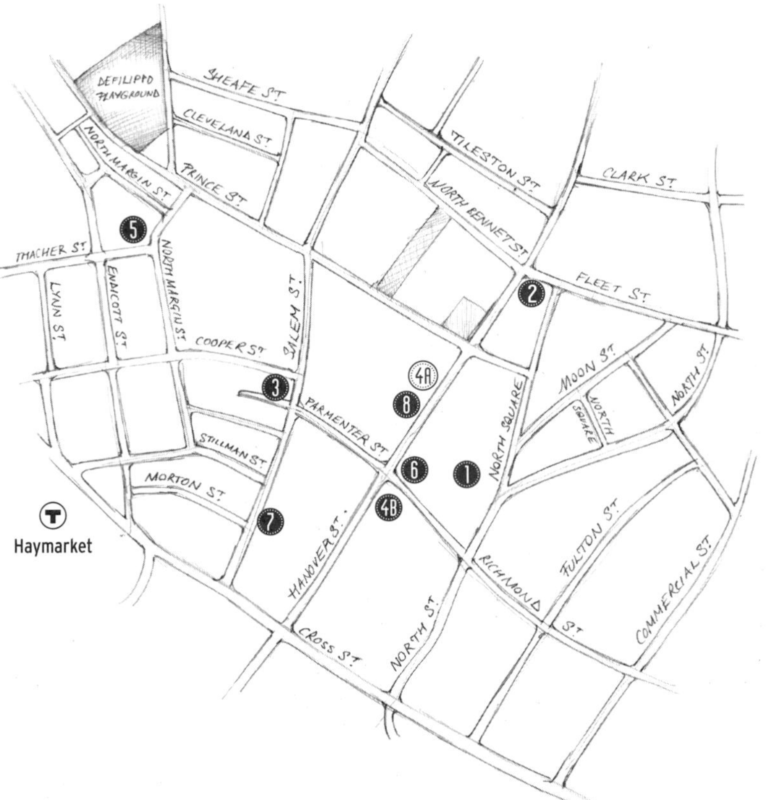

CARMEN TRATTORIA

Blissful Italian home cooking

33 North Square (between Moon and North) / +1 617 742 6421
carmenboston.com / Closed Mondays

Carmen Trattoria is tiny. So tiny, in fact, that "due to limited space" they cannot offer coffee or dessert so you don't linger after your meal and they can clear the table for the next group. It's about the size of a home's dining room and just as intimate. If you're socially anxious like me, intimate can sometimes translate to awkward. Friends, that is not the case here. The menu changes seasonally, so I can't guarantee the presence of the truffle pasta, but if you see it, order it. When sampled by my table of four, it caused a chain of reactions reminiscent of the deli scene in *When Harry Met Sally*. It probably did get a little awkward in there after that — but we were too blissed out to notice.

GIACOMO'S RISTORANTE

Generous portions to queue for

355 Hanover Street (between Fleet and Prince) / +1 617 523 9026
giacomosblog-boston.blogspot.com / Open daily

North End is packed with dependably awesome Italian restaurants. As such, my often hangry (hungry and angry) and impatient self seldom waits in line; I just roam until I find a free table. Giacomo's is the exception to my wandering ways. Known for its no-fuss Italian-American fare, they have a line out the door every night – whatever the weather – despite the fact that they're cash only and don't accept reservations. That tells you everything you need to know, but here's a bit more: the calamari is the best in the land and the zuppe di pesce with Fracomo sauce is a joy to behold. If ever there was proof that good things come to those who wait, Giacomo's is it.

L'OSTERIA

A taste of Tuscany

104 Salem Street (at Cooper Street) / +1 617 723 5844
losteria.com / Open daily

At L'Osteria, all the Italian staples are made masterfully, but I order the prosciutto-stuffed veal Valdostana every time even though I, without fail, leave half of its wonderfully melty perfection for my dining companions to finish for me. Although already full to bursting, they cannot resist, and I lead them all into an inevitable food coma. Sorry guys, but I have to keep my priorities straight when I'm here: if I ate the whole thing, I'd have no room for wine, which is a must at L'Osteria. I'm pretty sure that's a sin in Italy — and it's definitely a sin here, where full bottles are priced so that everyone can have their own. So cheers to overindulging, just this once.

MIKE'S PASTRY VS MODERN PASTRY

An epic Boston rivalry

Mike's Pastry: 300 Hanover Street (between Prince and Parmenter)
+1 617 742 3050 / mikespastry.com / Open daily
Modern Pastry: 257 Hanover Street (between Richmond and Cross)
+1 617 523 3783 / modernpastry.com / Open daily

The North End's winding streets are packed with pastry shops, but the cannoli landscape is famously centered around two classic contenders just a stone's throw away from one another on Hanover Street. The rivalry is as legendary as that of the Red Sox versus Yankees, but different in that this battle has no clear winner (wink, wink). Both are chaotic and crowded on any given night, but I would venture to say that Mike's dazzling storefront attracts a few more tourists, while the locals tend to go for the more modest Modern. In my professional opinion, the obviously correct cannoli choice is. . . both (duh!) — because why not? The taste test is as fun as the treats are delicious.

PIZZERIA REGINA

"Wicked good" pizza

11 1/2 Thacher Street (at North Margin Street)
+1 617 227 0765 / pizzeriaregina.com / Open daily

I was raised on Chicago deep-dish pizza restaurant greats, Lou Malnati's and Giordano's. I've lived in New York City, where many late nights ended with a slice of the famously foldable thin crust. I know pizza, you guys, and I'm dropping this bomb with complete confidence: Pizzeria Regina has the best pie this side of Italy. The wait may be long, the ambiance unremarkable and the service (endearingly) hostile, which means the pizza has to be worth it. Believe me, folks: it is. Though I'm typically a classic pepperoni girl, my top picks here are the shrimp scampi and spinach, and the St. Anthony's, a mouth-watering union of sausage, peppers and onions in a garlic sauce. You can't really go wrong – so long as you leave the skinny jeans at home.

SALUMERIA ITALIANA

Gourmet Italian groceries

151 Richmond Street (between Hanover and North)
+1 617 523 8743 / salumeriaitaliana.com / Open daily

I'm all about the yes. For most people, that's a great quality to have. But when combined with being easily inspired, shockingly impulsive and unjustifiably confident, it can be dangerous — particularly when it comes to cooking. I have made several questionable choices upon entering some of Boston's specialty grocers. Lobster-stuffed filet mignon wrapped in bacon for Valentine's Day? Absolutely! (Disaster ensued.) A seven-layer cheesecake served on a candy cane plate for Christmas? Shouldn't be a problem! (It was.) Salumeria Italiana is my safe space, where the glorious selection of cured meats, fresh pasta and aged cheese make it easy to achieve culinary excellence without getting carried away.

SHAKE THE TREE

Gifts for everyone, including yourself

67 Salem Street (between Cross and Stillman)
+ 1 617 742 0484 / shakethetreeboston.com / Open daily

I used to live near this funky hub of clothes, home goods and jewelry, and unknowingly walked past it several times before a colorful ceramic bowl caught my eye. Now it's my go-to spot for treasures I never knew I needed. Glass cloche ring holders and coffee-scented candles may seem superfluous to some, but they're just so nice when you have them. I once tore my apartment apart in search of the earrings I scored here. The wave of relief that rippled through me when I found them in my gym bag proves that however nonessential it may seem at first, a bauble from here can quickly join the ranks of one's most cherished pieces.

STANZA DEI SIGARI

Classic cigar parlor and liquor lounge

292 Hanover Street (between Prince and Parmenter)
+1 617 227 0295 / stanzadeisigari.com / Open daily

I'm not the cigar smoking type. However, seeing my friend Joe's eyes light up as he talked about Stanza dei Sigari, I knew it was somewhere special. In his words: "A bastion of a bygone era, Boston's only remaining cigar bar was once a 1920s speakeasy. Its sparse, dim lighting and piecemeal décor hold true to its illicit origins. Make no mistake, this isn't a men's club filled with the cacophony of politics and dirty jokes; Stanza welcomes all. With an extensive Scotch list, top quality cigars and a storied history, it's easily my favorite place to end the night." I'm already rethinking it: I might try a cigar after all.

food trucks

Meals on wheels

If I'm running, there are two possible explanations. The first is that I'm in extreme danger, and the second, I've heard the sweet song of an ice cream truck. As a child I had a superhuman ability to hear that particular melody and would bolt out the door before it was audible to the average ear. Not much has changed: when I spot a food truck that I like, I feel an almost supernatural surge of adrenaline that carries me right up to the hatch.

The Cookie Monstah is the new-and-improved version of my first love. Its handcrafted "chipwiches" pack a heaping scoop of cow-to-cone, farm fresh ice cream between two warm, gooey cookies of your choosing. Fellow chocoholics, rejoice: the classic chocolate chip has, in the words of the Monstah herself, "just enough dough to hold the chocolate together."

A friend of mine stylishly keeps her dish soap in a glass olive oil bottle, and I once accidentally made a soap-soaked grilled cheese. Upon my horrifying realization, I considered eating it anyway. My love for cheese runs that deep, so believe me when I say that **Roxy's Grilled Cheese** masters the classic. As a bonus, it also offers amped-up options that include guacamole, bacon and caramelized onions.

BON ME
Visit @bonme on Twitter for daily locations
+1 617 989 9804, bonmetruck.com

CLOVER
Visit website for daily locations, +1 617 395 0240
cloverfoodlab.com

ROXY'S GRILLED CHEESE
Visit @RoxysGrilledChz on Twitter for daily locations
+1 617 202 5864, roxysgrilledcheese.com

THE CHICKEN AND RICE GUYS
Visit website for daily locations, +1 617 903 8538
cnrguys.com

THE COOKIE MONSTAH
Visit website for daily locations, +1 617 615 6595
thecookiemonstah.com

Clover food truck doesn't need a song to get your attention: you can smell the rosemary fries from blocks away. Focusing on seasonal ingredients and hearty vegetarian options like sweet potato sandwiches, Clover has a cult following as substantial as its meat-free nosh.

Though the husband and wife duo behind **Bon Me** were inspired by the classic Vietnamese bánh mì sandwich, their version is decidedly non-authentic: you can order it filled with spice-rubbed chicken, Chinese BBQ pork, miso-braised pulled pork, or roasted soy and paprika tofu. Try it once and you'll crave it every day thereafter.

I was hesitant to try **The Chicken and Rice Guys**, because chicken and rice is the one thing I can cook myself. Or so I thought. Then I tried this NYC-inspired Halal truck and realized I can't cook chicken and rice after all. At least, not like this.

waterfront and downtown

As an ignorant eighteen-year-old, I moved to Boston envisioning a glamorous cosmopolitan lifestyle. The reality of the decidedly unglamorous college life was harsh and, in my opinion, consisted of too many nights spent on campus. I had many a beer-fueled breakdown where I'd belligerently point to the distant skyline and screech, "I want to be where the skyscrapers are!" To appease me, my annoyed friends squeezed into a cab one Saturday night and told the driver to take us "there," motioning toward the city lights. Cue my infinite despair: we were taken to Downtown Boston's Financial District, which on a weekend night is an absolute ghost town. It's all office buildings, franchised steakhouses and sleepy bars. Defeated, I bitterly vowed never to return. When I found myself working there years later, I was pleasantly surprised to discover that it's not only home to some of the most prestigious consulting companies, investment banks and law firms in the world, but also several eateries worthy of such a distinguished population.

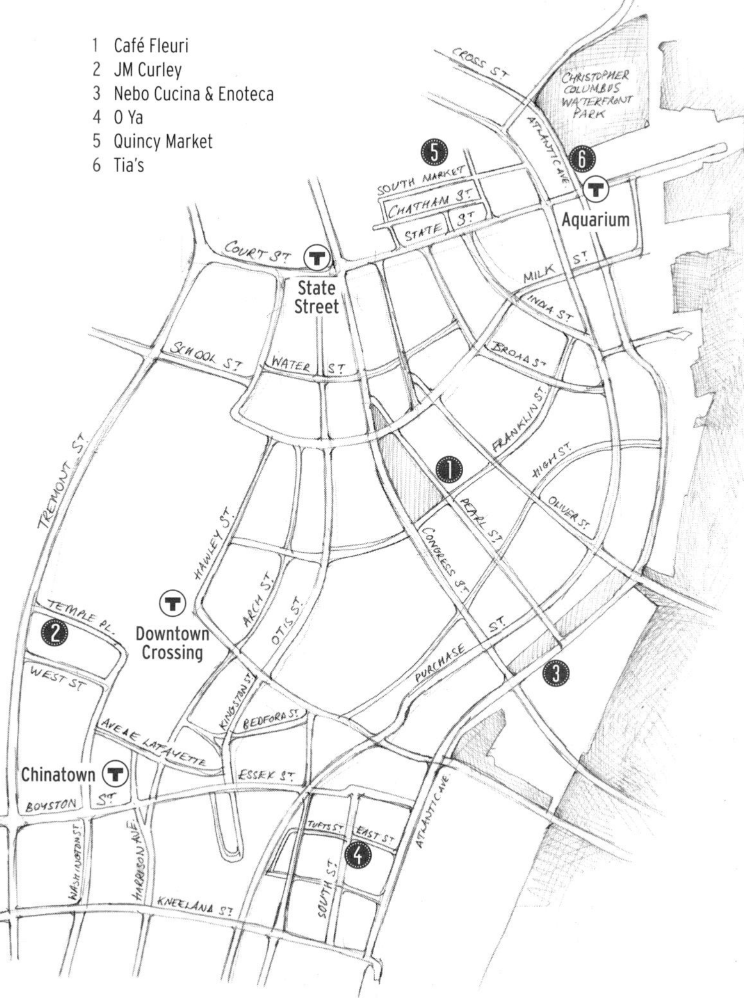

1 Café Fleuri
2 JM Curley
3 Nebo Cucina & Enoteca
4 O Ya
5 Quincy Market
6 Tia's
CROSS ST.
CHRISTOPHER COLUMBUS WATERFRONT PARK
ATLANTIC AVE.
SOUTH MARKET
CHATHAM ST.
STATE ST.
Aquarium
COURT ST.
State Street
MILK ST.
INDIA ST.
SCHOOL ST.
WATER ST.
BROAD ST.
FRANKLIN ST.
HIGH ST.
TREMONT ST.
PEARL ST.
OLIVER ST.
CONGRESS ST.
HAWLEY ST.
ARCH ST.
OTIS ST.
TEMPLE PL.
Downtown Crossing
ST.
WEST ST.
PURCHASE
KINGSTON ST.
BEDFORD ST.
AVE DE LAFAYETTE
Chinatown
ESSEX ST.
BOYLSTON ST.
WASHINGTON ST.
HARRISON AVE.
TUFTS ST.
EAST ST.
ATLANTIC AVE.
SOUTH ST.
KNEELAND ST.

CAFÉ FLEURI

All-you-can-eat chocolate dessert buffet

250 Franklin Street (between Pearl and Oliver) / +1 617 451 1900
langhamhotels.com/en/the-langham/boston/dining/cafe-fleuri
Open daily

Don't ask me why I'd been to Las Vegas — the land of the all-you-can-eat buffet — five times before I was of gambling age, because I don't know. What I do know though, is that I was burnt out on buffets. That is, I was until I had an epiphany beneath the lofty atrium ceilings of this ritzy restaurant in the Langham Hotel: combining chocolate with more chocolate is 100% foolproof. On Saturdays, Café Fleuri hosts a chocolate-dessert buffet featuring over 100 delicacies with varying levels of cocoa intensity and flavors, and on Sunday a selection from the Chocolate Bar is available during brunch. It's a wonderland of chocolate fountains, ice cream sundaes, lava cake and live jazz. In other words, heaven.

JM CURLEY

Juicy burgers for the night crowd

21 Temple Place (between Tremont and Washington) / +1 617 338 5333
jmcurleyboston.com / Open daily

Tattooed, bandana-wearing Chef Sam Monsour understands Bostonian needs. His menu is loaded with what I consider to be the best burgers in town. As if that's not enough, you can get them when you want them most: in the wee hours of the morning, après bar. He's also well versed in the ways we sometimes behave when we've been drinking, so he's added a list of "laws" to the menu that concludes with "just don't be a douchebag." I for one will follow any law if it means getting my hands on a luscious burger stuffed with gooey cheese and smothered in Russian dressing (serious eaters can get it "filthy Andy style," with slaw and fries inside the sandwich), accompanied by the world's most perfect shoestring fries. (Pssst: there's also a secret speakeasy in the back.)

NEBO CUCINA & ENOTECA

Italian sister act

520 Atlantic Avenue (between Congress and Pearl) / +1 617 723 6326
neborestaurant.com / Closed Sunday

My dietician friend Abby often gets so jazzed about the health benefits of a food that her mind hypnotizes her taste buds into believing it's yummy when it's not. As she told me about the zucchini lasagne at Nebo Cucina & Enoteca, I nodded enthusiastically while imagining a sad, paltry excuse for lasagne. Sometimes being wrong tastes so, so good, though. One bite and I pledged my allegiance to it as if my mom's had never existed. It's hearty, it's healthy and it bursts with the flavors of fresh zucchini and riccotta. Chefs/owners/sisters Carla and Christine have a knack for unexpected unions: while the food captures the essence of dining in an Italian home, the modern industrial décor makes it a hip destination for libations to boot.

O YA

Where sushi meets art

9 East Street (between South and Atlantic) / +1 617 654 9900
oyarestaurantboston.com / Closed Sunday and Monday

First my former boss introduced me to South End Buttery (see pg 65), making her responsible for around 5% of my body weight. Then she introduced me to O Ya, making her responsible for 25% of my depleted funds. Although there are only ten tables and a sushi counter, there are five chefs on any given night. You'll understand why when you experience the innovative sashimi. On the plate, each ornate piece dazzles like a rare jewel. On the tongue, it is no less sensational. The menu, which changes daily, is rooted in Japanese tradition but not shackled to it. Just heed this warning: it's not cheap. I can easily drop $150 each time I visit.

QUINCY MARKET

Bustling dining and shopping complex

4 South Market Street (between Merchants Row and Commercial)
+1 617 523 1300 / faneuilhallmarketplace.com / Open daily

Every weekend in the summer, the North End erupts in the wild
Feast festival where hundreds of pushcart vendors spill out into the
streets and men hoist up huge statues of saints in grand parades.
The atmosphere is that of a jovial street bazaar, so if you're around,
don't miss it. If you're here in another season, Quincy Market is the
next best thing. Some locals call it a tourist trap and glorified food
court, but I think the festive energy, huge array of peddlers, shops,
food vendors and vibrant street performers are like a shot of espresso.
If you enjoy a sensory overload every now and then, swing by and be
sure to check out Local Charm for jewelery from over 50 artists, as
well as Walrus and Carpenter for oysters.

TIA'S

Summertime happy hour hotspot

**200 Atlantic Avenue (between Christopher Columbus Park and State)
+ 1 617 227 0828 / tiaswaterfront.com / Open daily, April to October**

We don't need a groundhog to predict the arrival of spring: we have Tia's. This waterfront seafood restaurant has long been dubbed Boston's premier destination to bid the winter doldrums adieu and welcome the arrival of the sun. When Tia's overflows with party seekers and finance professionals alike, you'll know snow season is behind you. The three bustling patios showcase Boston Harbor and Christopher Columbus Park, providing the ultimate summery backdrop. Snagging a coveted table is never easy, but the chance to soak up some rays over steamed lobster, beer and frozen cocktails is one worth fighting for.

south end

A bustling gay, artistic and cultural community, South End is one of Boston's most vibrant neighborhoods. Uniform rows of quaint brick townhouses are peppered with nearly 30 lavishly green parks. Tremont Street, known as "Restaurant Row" to the locals, is a diner's haven where diverse upscale cuisine abounds. Prepare to gawk at the eclectic mishmash of independent shops, specializing in everything from couture dog accessories to urban garden supplies. Even when my wallet won't allow for a spending spree, South End makes a lovely setting for wistful window shopping, and I'm not just talking about the splurge-worthy merchandise. The men here are beyond devastating – both in terms of their looks and their complete disinterest in my gender. Le sigh.

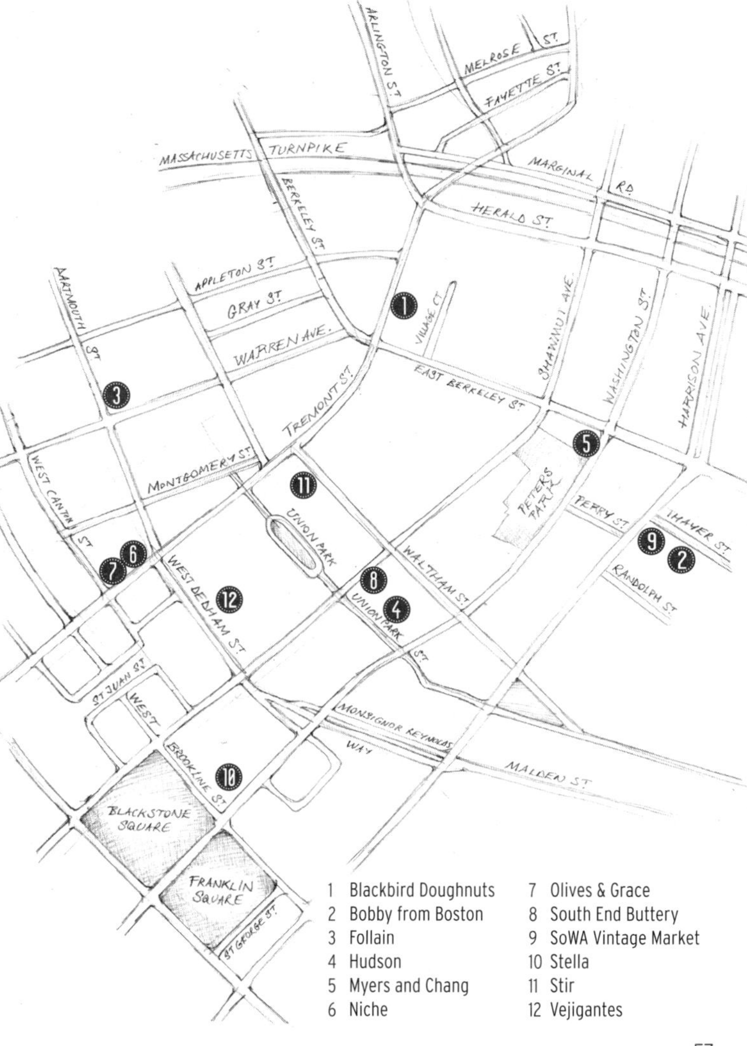

1 Blackbird Doughnuts
2 Bobby from Boston
3 Follain
4 Hudson
5 Myers and Chang
6 Niche
7 Olives & Grace
8 South End Buttery
9 SoWA Vintage Market
10 Stella
11 Stir
12 Vejigantes

BLACKBIRD DOUGHNUTS

Gourmet treats that will make you bid adieu to Dunkin

42 Tremont Street (between East Berkeley and Appleton)
+1 617 482 9000 / blackbirddoughnuts.com
Open Thursday–Sunday

Reading these reviews as if I were you, I realize that the woman you're likely envisioning is a massive glutton who eats everything put in front of her. I must confess this isn't the case: I do try to eat in moderation (my wardrobe has cost me quite a bit, and I can't afford a new one). While I pride myself on having some self-discipline, I admit that these doughnuts broke me, and continue to break me time and again. With an inventive selection of new flavors everyday (I've seen everything from French roast to pepperoni pizza), this is nirvana for the sweet teeth of Boston. Enter at your own risk, people.

BOBBY FROM BOSTON

A legend in the world of men's vintage

19 Thayer Street (at Harrison Street) / +1 617 423 9299
facebook.com/pages/Bobby-From-Boston / Closed Monday

Walking into Bobby From Boston, I feel like I've been granted rare access to the costume closet of *Mad Men*. Indeed, Bobby Garnett's acclaimed collection has provided the wardrobe for nearly 50 Hollywoods films. The entire shop is an escape to yesteryear, filled with classic menswear from the 1920s onward. There's also a soupçon of women's vintage threads, but I come here solely to outfit the men in my life, whether I'm snagging a watch for my brother or a funky Oxford for my bestie. It's a place that counts many fashion designers among its patronage, including regulars Ralph Lauren and Tom Ford: a fact I love to recite as my lucky recipient marvels over my spot-on gift.

FOLLAIN

Natural, small-batch beauty products

53 Dartmouth Street (at Warren Street) / +1 857 284 7078
shopfollain.com / Open daily

I once worked for a beauty website and the number of samples I received was absurd. They blanketed not only my desk, but, much to my boyfriend's dismay, every square inch of the bathroom counter, too. Even so, each time I popped into this haven of eco-friendly beauty products, I walked away with a bag brimming with goodies that I willingly purchased at full price. Follain features over 30 brands, all made in America and free of parabens, preservatives and synthetic chemicals. The collection includes products I consider to be game-changers, such as the Shamanuti charcoal cleanser, Josh Rosebrook nutrient day cream and May Lindstorm problem solver correcting mask. So, get thee to Follain. Your complexion will thank you.

HUDSON

Home accents in every style

12 Union Park Street (between Shawmut and Washington)
+1 617 292 0900 / hudsonboston.com / Open daily

I'm not proud of this, but my affinity for the wonderland of furniture and décor that is Hudson is best explained via anecdote. I once came here to purchase a wedding present for an ultra-hip couple. Choosing from the myriad eclectic home accents wasn't easy, but when I spotted a scaly gold picture frame I knew I'd hit a grand slam. Trendy yet timeless, it begged to hold a photo of the bride. So I bought it and sat it on my sideboard as I developed the photo. Do you see where this is heading? Each day it tormented me more until I admitted defeat: there was no way I could part with it. The moral of the story is that this is no place to buy a gift unless it's for your good self.

MYERS AND CHANG

Asian fusion at its finest

1145 Washington Street (at East Berkeley Street)
+1 617 542 5200 / myersandchang.com / Open daily

The small, sharable plates at Myers and Chang are "very personal interpretations" of Asian classics. Inspired by everything from Taiwanese comfort food to Southeast Asian street food, the menu varies, but the one consistency is fresh (and whenever an option, local) ingredients. The restaurant was born when Chef Joanne Chang proved to her husband, Christopher Myers, that one could eat Chinese food every night. This isn't the heavy, sloppy takeout to which he was accustomed: these are delicate, lightly sauced dishes. The wok-roasted mussels are absolutely mouth-watering, and another personal highlight is the wild mushroom lo mein, but it's tough to play favorites: everything is delicious.

NICHE

Urban garden supply

619 Tremont Street (between West Canton and Dartmouth)
+1 857 753 4294 / nicheboston.com / Closed Monday and Tuesday

Someone once told me, "If you want a baby, get a pet. If you want a pet, get a plant." Sage advice, but it implies that caring for a plant is the easiest of all. Not so. I am a former nanny and cat-owner, and while all children and felines left under my care remain very much alive, I have murdered an obscene amount of flora. My thumbs are not green, but once I step inside this bewitching emporium, my faith in my gardening skills is instantly restored. Luckily, shop owner Lindsey is happy to recommend the right plants for my space and to patiently explain how to care for them. 33rd time's the charm, right?

OLIVES & GRACE

Handcrafted, purposefully curated gifts

623 Tremont Street (between West Canton and Dartmouth)
+1 617 236 4536 / olivesandgrace.com / Open daily

If *The HUNT Guides* took the form of a tiny artisan gift shop, Olives & Grace would be it. Featuring the smallest brands with the biggest hearts, bright-eyed Sofi Madison calls her carefully chosen selection "a curtsy to the makers." Her charming little nook is filled with everyday items that have been turned into treasures by the power of thoughtful, small-batch production. From sriracha made with locally sourced peppers and aged in oak barrels, to rosemary mint grass-fed goat's milk soap, these are the types of gifts that can free you from the doghouse, win the heart of the dubious in-law and secure your spot as the star of the housewarming party in one fell swoop.

SOUTH END BUTTERY

Comfort food café

314 Shawmut Avenue (at Union Park Street) / +1 617 482 1015
southendbuttery.com / Open daily

Blame my former boss for the pounds you'll gain here. In our first email exchange, she suggested meeting at South End Buttery for an interview and wrote, "I'll be tempted to eat a grilled cheese sandwich, which is made with a block of cheese and three sticks of butter." I knew then that ours was a colleague match made in carb heaven, and the aforementioned sandwich, a divinely gooey devil made with Gruyère and aged cheddar, solidified our work relationship. I convinced myself that it was the peaceful ambiance and pleasant staff that kept me coming back. But that was buffoonery. You and I both know the real lure, and it rhymes with shrilled sleaze.

SOWA VINTAGE MARKET

Sunday market of eclectic vintage goods

460 Harrison Avenue (at Thayer Street)
+1 857 264 0932 / sowavintagemarket.com / Open Sunday

My first SoWa Vintage Market experience was bittersweet. Pro: I stumbled upon the spitting image of a Restoration Hardware cocktail table I'd been coveting for months going for a small fraction of the price I'd have otherwise paid. Con: I couldn't help but wonder how many other bonanzas I'd missed out on, wincing at all the former Sundays I spent naïvely sipping mimosas while someone snagged a bargain meant for me. Whether you're searching for a fur coat or a coffee table burnished with the glow of yesteryear, SoWa is chock-full of double-take inducing vintage pieces. Go, but know that every Sunday thereafter you will face serious FOMO (Fear Of Missing Out).

STELLA

Bustling avante-garde hotspot

1525 Washington Street (at Brookline Street)
+1 617 247 7747 / bostonstella.com / Open daily

A South End staple for the past 10 years, Stella is the incandescent star of Washington Street, its gleaming white interior always abuzz with welcoming energy. Even from a distance, the light burns bright, guiding a vibrant mix of locals to "shelter" (read: Martinis) like the Star of Bethlehem. Whether you come for dinner (the homemade gnocchi should do nicely), a midnight snack (the mushroom flatbread never fails) or a nightcap (if we're being real here, your last three drinks), the crowd is unfailingly fabulous. I especially love Stella for Sunday brunch, when it hums with the lively, whirling sound of clinking Champagne flutes and volcanic laughter.

STIR

The aspiring chef's delight

102 Waltham Street (at Tremont Street) / +1 617 423 7847
stirboston.com / Closed Sundays

As an Audrey Hepburn aficionado, I watch *Sabrina* more than any sane human should. Each time, by the film's end, my browser history contains searches for flights to Paris and courses at Le Cordon Bleu. At Stir, an enchanting cookbook shop with a demonstration kitchen, daily classes are put on by Boston's top chefs and range from $60 to $185. New regions are explored each night, allowing guests to conquer everything from boeuf bourguignon to sushi. Look for me – I'll be the one channeling Sabrina by "forgetting" to turn on the oven just so I can say, in my best French accent, "A woman happily in love, she burns the soufflé! A woman unhappily in love, she forgets to turn on the oven!"

VEJIGANTES

A taste of Puerto Rico in a casual, lively space

57 West Dedham Street (between Tremont and Shawmut)
+1 617 247 9249 / vejigantesrestaurant.com / Open daily

In every office, there are certain non-work-related topics everyone must familiarize themself with so as to avoid social alienation. Sometimes this topic is a TV show or movie. In my workspace, the topic was Vejigantes. Each of my officemates considered this authentic, low-key Puerto Rican joint a secret, and couldn't believe when the others knew about it too. Upon this discovery, all hope of productivity was immediately abandoned. A detailed conversation about mofongo, aranitas and paella ensued, sprinkled with squeals of excitement. I sulked all day, feeling left out because I'd never been there, and went that night. Every single thing was worthy of the hype, and with that it became our designated spot to TGIF.

game on

Where to watch Boston win

I would probably be met with resistance if I proclaimed that Boston's professional sports teams are the best in the land. So I won't. I'll just offer you the numbers, without commentary: since Y2K, Boston has claimed nine sports championships – more than any other city. Whether or not you'll admit that our teams are superior, walk into any of these bars and you'll see that the enthusiasm of our fans is unparalleled. To me, their endearingly riled-up reactions are as entertaining as the games themselves.

The legendary Fenway Park is the oldest baseball stadium in the country. The ultimate way to experience this historic icon is to head to **Bleacher Bar**, which sits beneath the seats in center field and features a giant window looking directly into the ballpark. CNN calls it "the most unique sports bar in the world," and I concur.

The Baseball Tavern is the next best thing: a fly ball's distance from Fenway, it has a roof deck with a panoramic view. Outdoor TV screens provide guests the opportunity to sunbathe and shout obscenities simultaneously. Don't be fooled by the name – it's not just for baseball. I saw our ice hockey team, the Bruins, win the Stanley Cup here and will "nevah fahget it."

For those willing to wait in line for a dive bar (and, believe it or not, many Bostonians are), try **Stats Bar & Grille**. Originally a local pub for Southie residents, it's become a hangout for trendy local singles thanks to gentrification. But the bar has retained its gritty character, which means there's something about this place that makes everyone inside attempt a *Good Will Hunting* impersonation.

In the South End, check out **Trophy Room**, a former sports bar for the gay crowd reimagined as an equally welcoming chef- and cocktail-driven spot with an elegant interior. The big hitter on the food menu is their spicy cauliflower buffalo "wing" dish that attracts patrons from all walks of life.

One of the oldest establishments in Boston, **The Red Hat** gives you everything you want from your friendly local watering hole, without a single frill. It's the ultimate traditional pub, and its 10-cent wing specials have been drawing crowds for over 100 years.

south boston and seaport

South Boston is no longer the South Boston you know from the movies. "Southie," as the locals call it, is a historically blue-collar Irish-Catholic neighborhood that has recently been colonized by young professionals who have renamed it "SoBo." The change is so drastic that infamous resident mobster Whitey Bulger probably wouldn't even recognize his former stomping grounds. In the nearby Seaport District, a hip new destination for the whole city, you'll find a sky-high row of ritzy restaurants towering over the water, offering sweeping harbor views. It's all glass and metal and neon lights, a strong departure from the little brick buildings to which we're otherwise accustomed. A few more blocks in and you'll find the labyrinth of colorful townhouses and time-honored Irish pubs often seen on screen: of note, L Street Tavern from *Good Will Hunting* and Murphy's Law of *Gone, Baby Gone*. A peculiar mix of scruffy Irish character and flashy modernity, South Boston is well worth the T ride.

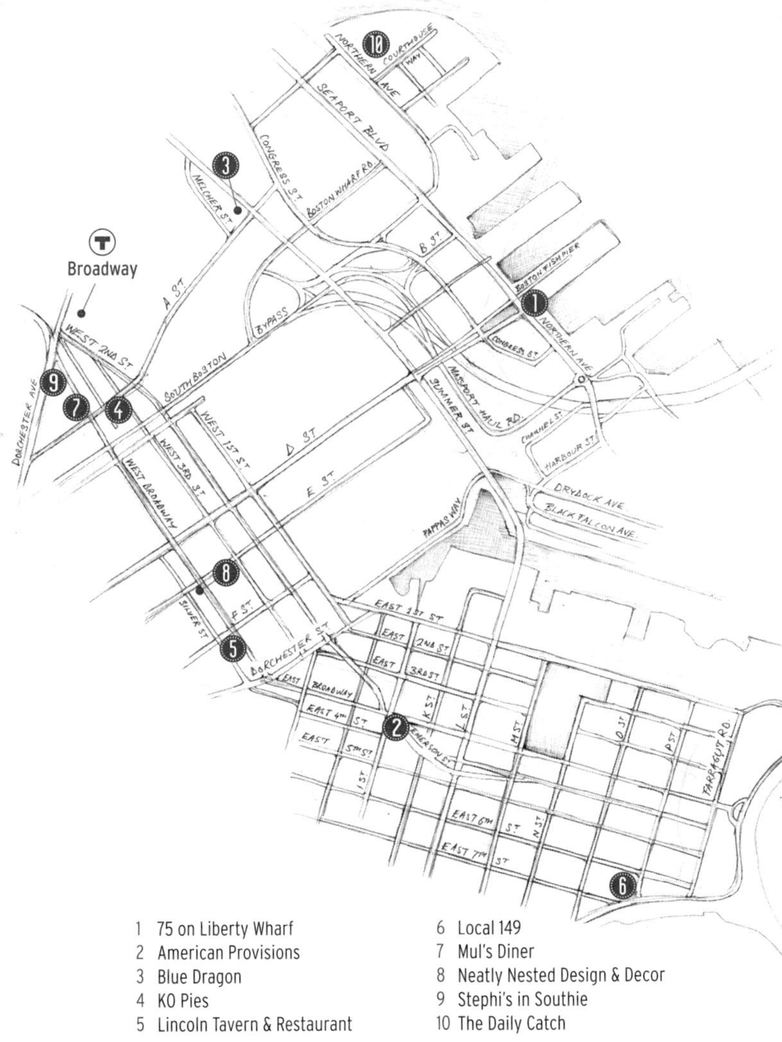

1 75 on Liberty Wharf
2 American Provisions
3 Blue Dragon
4 KO Pies
5 Lincoln Tavern & Restaurant
6 Local 149
7 Mul's Diner
8 Neatly Nested Design & Decor
9 Stephi's in Southie
10 The Daily Catch

75 ON LIBERTY WHARF

The little restaurant that could

220 Northern Avenue (at Boston Fish Pier) / +1 617 227 0480
75onlibertywharf.com / Open daily

When choosing a restaurant, you must prioritize desired attributes: do you want dramatic floor-to-ceiling windows with panoramic water views, or a comfy, intimate atmosphere? Do you want a swanky scene, or something casual? Dine al fresco and feel a pleasant cool breeze, or be snug as a bug, thawing out near a blazing fire? You can't have it all. Except here, that is. 75 on Liberty Wharf can grant all six wishes at once. This little wood-lined restaurant offers big views, the menu brims with New England pub favorites (the seafood stew is top notch), and the ocean-side patio is stocked with fire pits, heat lamps and plush, warm blankets. The Rolling Stones were wrong: you can always get what you want.

AMERICAN PROVISIONS

Artisanal farm-to-table grocery store

613 East Broadway (at I Street) / +1 617 269 6100
americanprovisions.com / Open daily

I often find myself in the land of dinner limbo. Do I want to cook? Absolutely not. Do I want to go out? Ugh, not really. Am I hungry? Starving. When this scenario arises, there is but one solution: American Provisions. With an emphasis on local brands, they offer mind-blowingly fresh-tasting gourmet frozen pizzas and homemade ice cream, both of which require little effort but make me feel that my meal has been prepared by my very own chef. Only when it comes from this friendly little shop can a supper of pizza and ice cream feel like a nourishing and health-conscious choice. I also love their luscious selection of fresh fruits, veggies and handmade cheese, all sourced by small family farms.

BLUE DRAGON

Bold and contemporary gourmet Asian

324 A Street (between Melcher and Summer) / +1 617 338 8585
ming.com/blue-dragon.htm / Closed Sunday

Chef Ming Tsai's first venture, Blue Ginger, is a half hour outside of Boston. I was happy to endure the long T ride, smugly assuring my companions that the glorious East-meets-West cuisine was worth the trek. When sister restaurant Blue Dragon opened in Boston proper, the heavens parted, the angels sang and all was well in the world. The garlic-sake clams with udon noodles are, to put it colloquially, straight fire; the buttermilk tempura fried chicken is absolutely unreal, as is the sake-miso butterfish. Finish off with The Cookie, a deep-dish indulgence served warm and topped with ice cream and soy caramel, which I cannot describe without using profanity.

KO PIES

Traditional Aussie meat and veggie pies

87 A Street (at West 3rd Street) / +1 617 269 4500
kocateringandpies.com / Closed Sunday

I've been on dates with two Australians, and, well, it turns out I just don't get Australian men. Their approach to romance boggles my mind, as does their affinity for meat pies. Have some meat. Have some potatoes. Have some pie. 'Why combine all three?', I'd find myself wondering every time I walked past KO Pies, an Aussie-inspired quick-serve joint. When the question crossed my mind for the 17th time, I decided to find out. After one bite of the Classic (lean ground beef cooked with sweet white onions in peppered gravy), I now have a profound appreciation for those from down under — or at least, for their food.

LINCOLN TAVERN & RESTAURANT

South Boston's star attraction

425 West Broadway (between F and Dorchester) / +1 617 765 8636
lincolnsouthboston.com / Open daily

You need to go to Lincoln Tavern & Restaurant and you need to order the Kobe sliders. Grilled to perfection and topped with bacon aioli and a sunny-side up quail egg, these little burgers are legendary. The expansive space and soaring ceilings of this spot effectively thwart cabin fever, so on the weekend, many come for brunch and then lounge all day. The space can hold 300 thirsty bodies, and it regularly does. Though the lively crowd is always loud and keeps the wait staff on their toes, even those who complain about the service continue to turn up every week. The power of the Kobe slider compels them.

LOCAL 149

A Southie neighborhood pub unlike the others

149 P Street (at East 6th Street) / +1 617 269 0900
local149.com / Open daily

Much can be said about South Boston's ongoing metamorphosis. Each time the subject arises I think of a quote from a Southie native that has stayed with me. He summed it all up with such admirable brevity, and in a most exemplary Boston accent: "We got yah wine drink-ahs now." Yes, we do – and Local 149 is where they gather. With savory fare and innovative cocktails, this one's for the yuppies – and the locals aren't even upset about it. In a neighborhood where mediocre pub food is the norm, perfectly executed dishes like hand-cut steak tartare, roasted flounder roulade and handmade ricotta gnocchi, and drinks like the Southie Rosé (Gruet Brut Rosé, grapefruit and créme de pêche) are deviations welcomed by all.

MUL'S DINER

Breakfast worth getting up early for

75 West Broadway (at A Street) / +1 617 268 5748
No website / Open daily

I wouldn't recommend talking to early-morning me. With limbs that feel like they're filled with sand and a brain that's only operating at about 20%, I'm certainly not playing with a full deck. Worse, I can be straight-up mean. There's only one way to guarantee that Morning Brittany is moderately pleasant: the crème brûlée French toast from Mul's Diner. If you hate everyone who smiles before 9 a.m., this place is where it's at. The décor is retro, the staff is polite but not unreasonably cheery, and that crème brûlée French toast is, well — it's crème brûlée French toast. Must I go into further detail? The other ingredient necessary for me to have a somewhat-sunny disposition is bottomless coffee, which they happily provide.

NEATLY NESTED DESIGN & DECOR

Darling vintage furnishings

373 West Broadway (at E Street) / +1 609 923 4459
neatlynesteddecor.com / Open daily

There are times when I suffer from extreme delusions of affluence. The most treacherous financial foxhole of all, for me, is furniture, especially pieces whose purpose is purely aesthetic. I'm looking at you, early-20th-century steel café barstools — you are gorgeous and I love you, but you are incredibly uncomfortable. Danielle at Neatly Nested Design & Decor is my ultimate enabler: she scours the planet for the coolest vintage finds, spiffs 'em up, and sells them at very fair prices. If the object of your affection isn't already awaiting you, she takes personal requests and is more than willing to hunt down options for you at trade shows and public markets.

STEPHI'S IN SOUTHIE

Boston's bubbly brunch

130 Dorchester Avenue (between West Broadway and Silver)
+1 617 345 5495 / stephisinsouthie.com / Open daily

Stephanie's on Newbury, one of Boston's most well-known and beloved restaurants, has two offshoot locations: all three are lovely and offer sophisticated comfort food – just thinking about the delectable shaved black forest ham they use in their Eggs Benedict makes my mouth water, and the hearty Cobb salad is second to none. But out of the three branches, I always prefer going to Stephi's in Southie. It gets my vote because it's the one that offers Bubble Service: $24 for a bottle of Prosecco plus peach, orange, grapefruit and cranberry juices for mixing. When I found out about it I thought it had to be a mistake. That's almost 12 mimosas for the price of two. But it's not a mistake. After this groundbreaking discovery, I actually shed tears of joy.

THE DAILY CATCH

Sicilian seafood and skyline views

2 Northern Avenue (at Courthouse Way) / +1 617 772 4400
thedailycatch.com/seaport / Open daily

This oceanfront restaurant offers a total escape from the hustle and bustle of urban life. Though the spectacular panoramic view of the city skyline assures me that I'm still very much in Boston, the patio is just feet from the cool water of the Boston Harbor, giving it an open-air ambiance that brings me right back to serene summers spent on Nantucket Island. The fact that the Sicilian-style seafood and pasta, comprised of Italian with French, Arab, Greek and Spanish influences, can hold a candle to the atmosphere says a lot. Do not be daunted by the bizarre look of the tinta di calamari, a homemade pasta drenched in pitch black squid ink; all who try it are immediately converted to its cult.

hotspots for new england fare

When in Bahstan, eat lobstah rolls and chowdah

ATLANTIC FISH CO.
761 Boylston Street (at Ring Road), +1 617 267 4000
atlanticfishco.com, open daily

B&G OYSTERS
550 Tremont Street (at Waltham Street)
+1 617 423 0550, bandgoyster.com, open daily

JAMES HOOK
15 Northern Avenue (at Atlantic Avenue), +1 617 423 5501
jameshooklobster.com, open daily

NEPTUNE OYSTER
63 Salem Street (at Morton Street), +1 617 742 3474
neptuneoyster.com, open daily

ROW 34
383 Congress Street (between Stillings and Boston Wharf)
+1 617 553 5900, row34.com, open daily

I once made the mistake of ordering a lobster roll outside of Boston. Years later, I stupidly did the same with clam chowder. Two words, friends: NEVAH AGAIN. Be forewarned that once you experience these delicacies at these destinations, you shouldn't bother eating them elsewhere again.

Seafood restaurants are as ample as Red Sox caps in our fair city, and you can find a decent lobster roll on every corner. But do you want a decent lobster roll? Nay, you want the perfect lobster roll, and for that **Island Creek Oyster Bar** (see pg 16) and **Neptune Oyster** are the clear frontrunners. In some of Boston's sleekest surrounds, the former serves up a shining paragon of traditional lobster roll excellence. The latter is a tiny seafood bar with a giant lobster roll, and all you need to know is that you must get it Connecticut style, which means drenched in butter. I sense that you flinched but listen to me: do it. I'm positive this is what they serve in heaven, and it's worth every single calorie.

While Island Creek boast's Boston's best traditional lobster roll and Neptune Boston's best buttery one, make a rezzie at **Row 34** if you want to try both kinds in one sitting.

During Boston's bone-chilling winters, chicken noodle soup sometimes just ain't enough. Let's talk clam chowder. Contrary to what some may think, thicker does not mean better. In fact, it usually indicates too much flour, which makes the chowder bland. The real stuff, any Boston foodie will tell you, has a thin base that's both light and rich at once, with loads of sensationally tender clams, pork, onions and potatoes. This in mind, **B&G Oysters** and **Atlantic Fish Co.** make the rest look like sad gray sludge. At B&G, bacon lardons and spicy croutons keep things smoky and zesty at once. As for Atlantic, all you need to know is: get the bread bowl.

If you're feeling casual and/or looking for chowder and lobster on-the-go, **James Hook** is a tiny family-owned hut that's legendary for its simple approach to Boston staples. The food is always fresh, but never fancy.

charlestown

somerville

As partial as I am to the vintage homes of Back Bay,
I must say I'm intimately familiar with the rental scene
in Charlestown as well, due to many hours spent
dreamily browsing the web after a night out at one of the
neighborhood's many award-winning restaurants.
Even older than Boston itself, Charlestown is a gorgeous
time portal, and each time I visit I am completely seduced
by the contrast between history-rich landmarks like the
Bunker Hill Monument and the new generation of fresh-
faced young professionals who have migrated to join the
classically Irish-American population (likewise in neighboring
Somerville, which was part of Charleston until 1842).
Hitting the pavement, or cobblestone, as it were, is a favorite
pastime of longtime natives and newcomers alike, as the
colonial streets are sprinkled with antique lanterns and
scores of noteworthy shops and restaurants. Just know that
the charm levels here are off the charts, and you might find
yourself drawn into an open house like a moth to a flame.

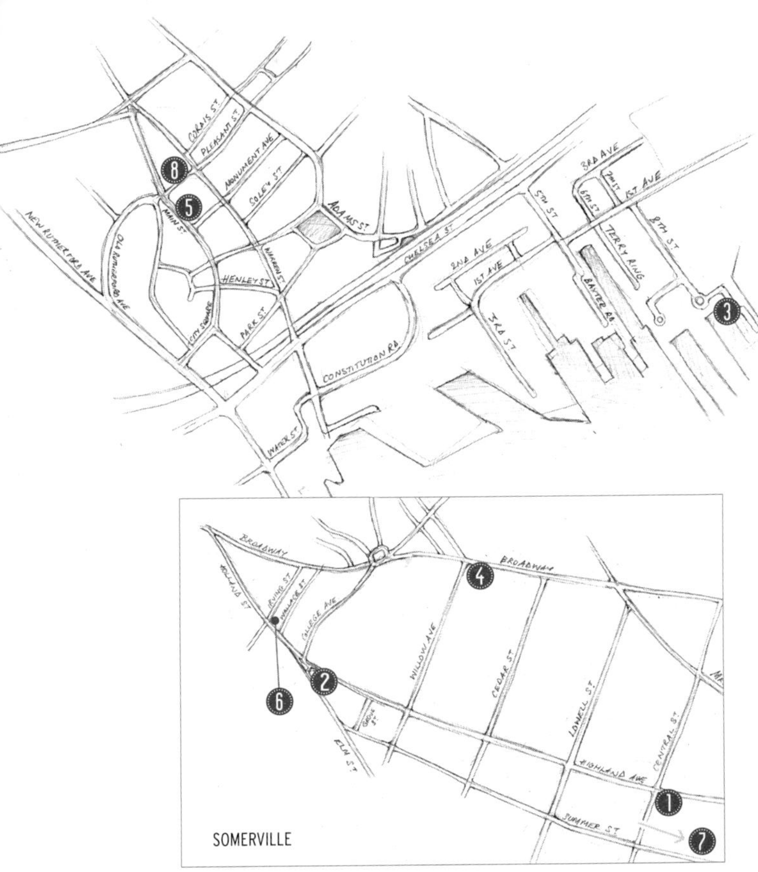

1	Highland Kitchen	5	Tangierino Chophouse and Tapas
2	Magpie	6	The Boston Shaker
3	Pier 6	7	The Neighborhood Restaurant & Bakery (off map)
4	Sound Bites	8	The Warren Tavern

HIGHLAND KITCHEN

A Southern-inspired scene worthy of the hype

150 Highland Avenue (at Central Street) / +1 617 625 1131
highlandkitchen.com / Open daily

I once wrote a piece about where Boston chefs dine when they're off duty; Highland Kitchen was a recurring entry. With bluegrass tunes and rainbow twinkle lights, it's a hip drinking scene for sure, but many would also line up for the seasonal American comfort food, and the no-reservations policy often means they have to. I now go before I'm hungry, put my name in and indulge in an elderflower margarita at the bar. By the time I've polished off one or two, my appetite starts to surface just as I'm being seated. Definitely order the Caribbean-style curried goat stew, a remarkably tender union of meat, sticky coconut rice, plantains, carrots and potatoes. You don't have to be a chef to see why they all love it here.

MAGPIE

A brick and mortar Etsy

416 Highland Avenue (between College and Grove)
+ 1 617 623 3330 / magpie-store.com / Open daily

The first time I heard about Magpie, it was described as a "hipster craft store." I pictured it as a real-life *Saturday Night Live* skit of a pompous art store with exasperated staff members who'd roll their eyes as they informed customers that scrapbooking should be done on found objects instead of paper nowadays. I was delighted when that vision wasn't the reality. Here, you'll find everything from a birthday card so quirkily personal that it needs no gift to accompany it to a morning coffee mug so cute that you'll stop hitting snooze. And the employees? The polar opposite of condescending.

PIER 6

Fresh fish and photo ops to boot

1 8th Street (at end of pier) / +1 617 337 0054
pier6boston.com / Open daily

I'm a sucker for a beautiful sunset and as my Instagram page attests,
I don't think I've ever visited Pier 6 without snapping a photo of the
waterside skyline scene. Situated beside the world's oldest commissioned
naval ship afloat, the *U.S.S. Constitution* (where The Freedom Trail ends,
see pg 128), Pier 6 has floor-to-ceiling glass sliding doors and an airy
patio exhibiting a view of the Boston skyline. The fresh seafood is always
delectable, and I struggle not to order the perfectly seared scallops every
time, although equally tempting are the lightly fried oysters topped with
crispy bits of celery and dressed in house-made tartar sauce. Go, and
don't forget your camera.

SOUND BITES

Cure-all breakfast joint

**704 Broadway (between Willow and Josephine) / +1 617 623 8338
soundbitesrestaurant.com / Open daily**

In college, my friends and I spent many nights drinking whiskey and attempting to learn to play the guitar. I was profoundly bad at both. Though these were very mellow evenings, excessive consumption of Jameson assured we would wake up with wretched hangovers. Sound Bites was our trusty solution. Waffles with a side of fries were usually enough to clear the foggiest of heads, but the deluxe breakfast sandwich was reserved for those OMG-seriously-never-touching-another-drop-again mornings. Served on a double toasted English muffin with tomato and grilled onions, with a sweet stack of pumpkin pancakes on the side, even today I can count on it to cure what ails me and then some.

TANGIERINO CHOPHOUSE AND TAPAS

A Moroccan sensory experience

83 Main Street (at Monument Avenue) / +1 617 242 6009
tangierino.com / Open daily

If ever you want to visit a far-off land but can't afford the airfare, consider this sultry Moroccan chophouse. The magic happens the moment you enter its exotic, swirling world of bejeweled lanterns, flowing tapestries and belly dancers. Drenched in opulence, the space boasts Arabic beats and a seductive hookah lounge that make it stylish enough to be a cocktail destination on its own. It would be a tragedy not to sample the array of North African dishes like the charbroiled rack of lamb with vibrant spices or nibble on tapas such as savory shrimp with feta or fork-tender braised boneless short ribs.

THE BOSTON SHAKER

Inspiring barware for your inner mixologist

69 Holland Street (between Irving and Wallace) / +1 617 718 2999
thebostonshaker.com / Open daily

When imbibing at a craft cocktail bar, I always find myself ignoring my companions and gaping at the bartenders as they churn out four or five artfully garnished masterpieces in minutes. Watching them leaves me yearning to be on the other side of the bar conducting a cocktail orchestra of my own. At The Boston Shaker, a haven of muddlers, juicers and strainers, I am equally inspired. Coconut bottle openers and ceramic tiki mugs can take any barbecue to the next level, and wooden mallets and hand-stitched cloth bags ensure you look painfully cool as you crush ice. Everything in here calls for a party I want to host.

THE NEIGHBORHOOD RESTAURANT & BAKERY

Breakfast for economical eaters with big appetites

25 Bow Street (between Wesley Park and Walnut) / +1 617 623 9710
theneighborhoodrestaurant.com / Open daily

Everyone has one complaint about this laid-back Portuguese family-run diner: the tables are too small to accommodate all the food that comes free with your $12 entree. In addition to your (very American-sized) main, you get a choice of Cream of Wheat or the fruit of the day (usually a grapefruit half or a baked apple), plus orange juice, everlasting coffee, fresh, buttered bread and warm corn muffins. The coconut French toast is a crowd favorite, but I always order #27: steak and eggs, with the addictively seasoned tips cooked medium rare. Every time, they're a paragon of doneness done right.

THE WARREN TAVERN

Iconic pub oozing with colonial charm

2 Pleasant Street (between Main and Warren) / + 1 617 241 8142
warrentavern.com / Open daily

I love that Boston is home to so many establishments that are steeped in history. I only recently discovered The Warren Tavern, but it's been here since 1780 and is one of the oldest taverns in America. Paul Revere was a regular, as was George Washington, whose funeral speech was given here. The antiqued atmosphere may take center stage, but the classic pub fare and drinks are top-notch supporting acts. Although they are famous for their burgers (especially the signature Tavern burger, with house garlic-herb cream cheese and honey dijon), I'd be remiss not to mention the perfectly-seasoned wings.

BOSTON AFTER DARK:
laugh it off

Where to sit down for stand up

Jay Leno. Amy Poehler. Conan O'Brien. Mindy Kaling. Steve Carell. This city has churned out so many comedians, I often wonder if humor is embedded in the genetic code of Bostonians. It's either that or the result of daily interactions with the city's abundance of outrageous characters, from the "urban outdoorsman" on Newbury Street who freestyles songs about passersby, to the 75-year-old man in full disco attire who has spent every waking moment since 1985 at dive bar Daisy Buchanan's. Nature or nurture, one thing's for sure: we're funny here.

Audience involvement is the name of the game at **Improv Asylum** and **Improv Boston**, where spectators yell out keywords that become the central themes of on-the-spot skits. My friends and I once arrived late, shocked to discover that the entire front row was vacant. We stopped counting our lucky stars shortly thereafter: these are the hot seats, and occupying them means sacrificing yourself to the room for entertainment value. For the brave, though, there's truly nothing funnier than seeing every triviality of your life played out in a snide little musical.

IMPROV ASYLUM
BOSTON
COMEDY ARTS
FESTIVAL
ImprovBoston

Dick Doherty's Comedy Den, where Dane Cook got his start, is located below the infamously sloppy Howl at the Moon Dueling Piano Bar. Pregame at one to enhance your experience at the other – either way works.

On the third floor of a Chinese restaurant, Harvard Square's **The Comedy Studio** serves deadly scorpion bowls that have the power to make anything funny, and at $10 admission for a two hour show, the prices can't be beat.

If it's Wednesday, snag one of 300 seats at **Laugh Boston** for the Boston Accents show, which showcases the city's unique brand of comedy by featuring some of the finest Boston-bred comedians, from newbies to legends.

BOSTON AFTER DARK:
cocktail bars

Sophisticated sips

ALIBI
215 Charles Street (between Fruit and Cambridge)
+1 857 241 1144, libertyhotel.com/food_and_drink/
alibi_room.html, open daily

BACKBAR
7 Sanborn Court (at Washington Street)
+1 617 718 0249, backbarunion.com, open daily

EASTERN STANDARD KITCHEN & DRINKS
528 Commonwealth Avenue (between
Brookline and Kenmore), +1 617 532 9100
easternstandardboston.com, open daily

LIQUID ART HOUSE
100 Arlington Street (between Stuart and Piedmont)
+1 617 457 8130, liquidarthouse.com, open daily

THE GALLOWS
1395 Washington Street (between Union Park
and Pelham), +1 617 425 0200
thegallowsboston.com, open daily

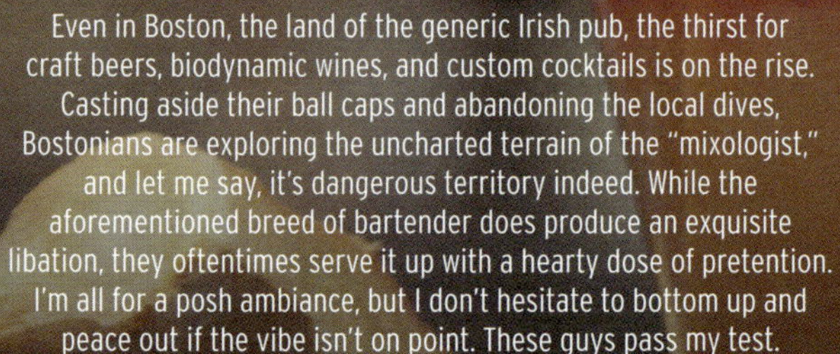

Even in Boston, the land of the generic Irish pub, the thirst for craft beers, biodynamic wines, and custom cocktails is on the rise. Casting aside their ball caps and abandoning the local dives, Bostonians are exploring the uncharted terrain of the "mixologist," and let me say, it's dangerous territory indeed. While the aforementioned breed of bartender does produce an exquisite libation, they oftentimes serve it up with a hearty dose of pretention. I'm all for a posh ambiance, but I don't hesitate to bottom up and peace out if the vibe isn't on point. These guys pass my test.

Alibi is the aptly-named bar at The Liberty Hotel (see pg 9), a 19th-century prison that is now one of Boston's most distinctive properties. Inside its colossal stone façade, Boston's bleary-eyed elite can be found trying not to spill their brimming martinis on their classy cocktail attire. In a city that doesn't exactly specialize in glamorous nightlife, this is the go-to destination for serious swank.

Liquid Art House is the ultimate conversation piece: a wonderfully upscale bar with a rotating art exhibit inside. With subdued music, dim lighting, and a fascinating array of ever-changing artwork, the distractions are minimal aside from the feast of eye candy, so as to encourage the rarity that is human interaction. Speaking of humans, the ones you'll find here are often of the painfully stylish variety; I once spotted a woman sipping a Martini here in an iridescent dress made entirely of cellophane.

It's all about the custom cocktails at **Backbar** – name a spirit and a fruit you like and let the bartender take it from there. That said, my tipple of choice here the piña pepper colada, served with a bell pepper and coconut pastis sorbet, can be ordered right off the menu.

The Gallows is a quaint little joint that's not afraid to pass some bold cocktails across the bar. The Brazen Bull, with jalapeño and scotch bonnet-infused vodka, will wake me up from any coffee crash. I like to follow that up with something on the softer side, like the Sicilian Smash, made with blood orange vodka and topped with sparkling cava.

And when Boston's blistery cold makes bar hopping unthinkable, **Eastern Standard Kitchen & Drinks** is my one-stop shop for adventurous seasonal cocktails, complete with egg whites and house made bitters. My personal favorite is Prospect Park, a killer riff on the rye-based Red Hook cocktail, that I perpetually regret the morning after.

cambridge

Grab a seat near the window on the Red Line as you zip over the Longfellow Bridge to cross the Charles River. After a few short minutes of taking in the lovely skyline view, you'll find yourself in Cambridge. Named after the prestigious school in England, Cambridge is famously home to two prominent institutions of our own, Harvard University and Massachusetts Institute of Technology. It's exciting to simply breathe the academic air here — which I swear smells like old books — knowing you're sharing it with some of the world's greatest minds. Cambridge has not only nurtured seven presidents including Barack Obama and John F. Kennedy, but also Edwin "Buzz" Aldrin of NASA's Apollo 11 mission, Facebook founder Mark Zuckerberg, and Elle Woods of *Legally Blonde*, even if she is fictional. It comes as no surprise then, that there are so many genius shops and restaurants here as well.

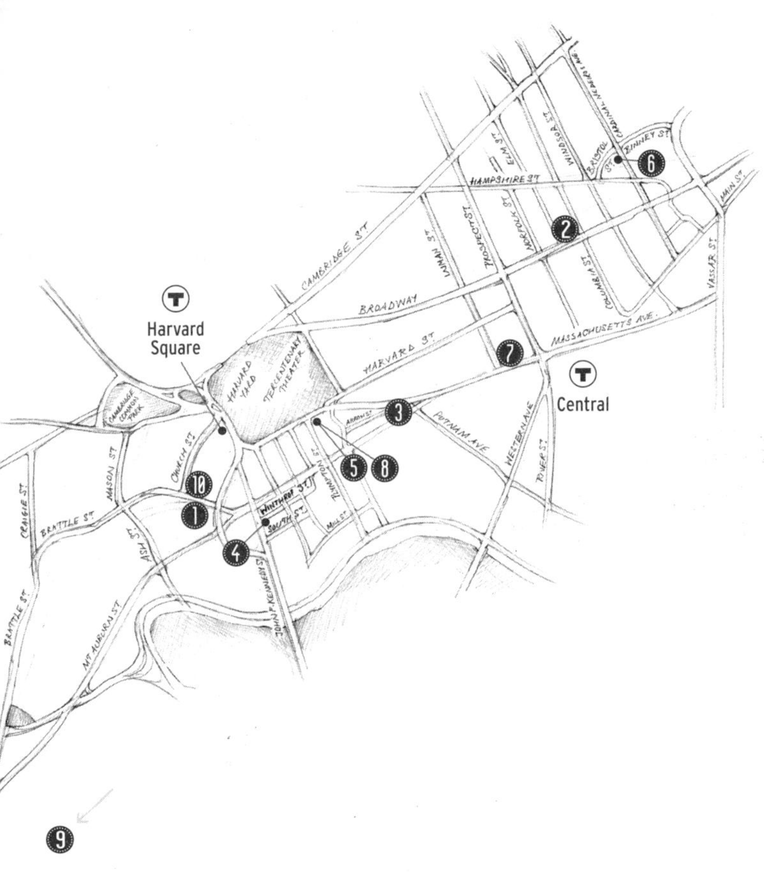

1	Alden & Harlow	6	Hungry Mother
2	Bondir	7	Life Alive
3	Follow the Honey	8	Mr. Bartley's Gourmet Burgers
4	Forty Winks	9	Sofra Bakery (off map)
5	Grolier Poetry Book Shop	10	The Tannery

ALDEN & HARLOW

New American cuisine in industrial-chic digs

40 Brattle Street (between Brattle Square and Story)
+1 617 864 2100 / aldenharlow.com / Open daily

A friend and I once dropped off a ravenous buddy here to put our names down while we parked the car. We walked in a few minutes later to find that he was already seated and had ordered the entire brunch menu. Though certainly shocked, I can't say I was mad about it. Everything from the cheesy smoked grits to the kale salad was delectable. Our umpteen entrees were accompanied by several bubbly mimosas, and by the time we polished off our last bite we were loving the upbeat atmosphere so much that we decided to stay for drinks at the bar. A few hours later, the same ambitious orderer announced that he was hungry again, so the three of us shared the chicken fried rabbit with bleu cheese and chili oil — a crispy, creamy treat that I count among the top five dishes I've ever eaten.

BONDIR

Farm-to-table French sans attitude

279A Broadway (between Elm and Columbia) / +1 617 661 0009
bondircambridge.com / Closed Tuesday

I'll happily endure less-than-perfect service in the name of a glorious dish, but I don't have to here because Bondir gets it just right. The maître d' is as as warm as the crackling fireplace, upon which he will warm your jacket before helping you into it at the end of your meal. That's just a bonus. Let's talk about the food. The menu changes daily based on the availability of local ingredients, and every time I eat a vegetable here it's as if I'm trying it for the first time, reveling in how magnificent it can be. Though I'm usually the last person to order chicken, I must say it is always sensational here: I know I can recommend it, no matter how it's prepared that day.

FOLLOW THE HONEY

Buzzworthy honey shop and tasting bar

**1132 Massachusetts Avenue (at Arrow Street) / +1 617 945 7356
followthehoney.com / Open daily**

Short on fruits and veggies one day, my mom offered me a spoonful of peanut butter drizzled with honey to hold me over until dinner. I savored every lick, and from that day on it was a hellish ordeal to get me to eat anything else. Follow the Honey's owner, Mary, is equally enthralled by the majestic amber substance that is honey. Her shop sells raw, untreated honeys from all over the world, which she offers on tap, dispensed into mason jars. Last time, I selected the lavender honey and a truffle honey, employing all my self-discipline to leave the lime flavor for my next visit.

Overhaul your underwear drawer

56 John F. Kennedy Street (between South and Winthrop)
+1 617 492 9100 / shopfortywinks.com / Open daily

They're called unmentionables, but friends Meredith and Rachel couldn't help themselves. One night over cocktails, they began to gripe. The cute undies weren't comfortable; the comfortable ones weren't cute. They were fed up and knew there had to be better options than what they were seeing. So they decided to make a go of it. Their store, Forty Winks, is a one-stop shop for fashionable lingerie that feels good, too, and they feature beautiful delicates from luxury brands like Cosabella and Stella McCartney in rare sizes at both ends of the spectrum. Looks like we can get back to grumbling about the male species when we drink. Oddly enough, we encounter a similar quandary there: the cute ones give you the most trouble.

GROLIER POETRY BOOK SHOP

The nation's oldest purveyor of poetry

**6 Plympton Street (at Massachusetts Avenue) / +1 617 547 4648
grolierpoetrybookshop.org / Closed Sunday and Monday**

Nestled in the shadow of Harvard Book Store, this enchanting shop contains a prolific array of quaint juxtapositions. It's the size of a closet, but as bright as a summer garden. Well-worn wooden shelves heave with 15,000 brand new poetry books in shiny sleeves, all neatly arranged. The clerk seemed hostile at first, her query about how I chanced upon this gem sounding more like an accusation — but only a moment later was revealed to be a skittish chatterbox, telling me about her fashion blog as she toyed with her fraying sweater. Even for people who aren't poetry fanatics, this romantic little nook is magic: a fairy tale come to life.

HUNGRY MOTHER

Farm fresh Southern feasting

233 Cardinal Medeiros Avenue (at Bristol Street) / +1 617 499 0090
hungrymothercambridge.com / Closed Monday

However odd it might be to start off by detailing the décor in the restrooms, I feel it serves as a paradigm for the ethos of the restaurant at large. One is wallpapered in pages from Julia Childs' *Mastering the Art of French Cooking*, the other with Mary Randolph's *The Virginia Housewife*. Accordingly, the cuisine here is simplistically Southern – grits and cornbread abound, but are meticulously prepared and presented in a way that feels distinctly French. I still rave about the cornmeal catfish I had here once, but you should note that the menu is ever evolving. The boiled peanuts are one constant though, and a must to start. Wash them down with an inspired apéritif and let intuition guide you from there.

LIFE ALIVE

Earthy eats for even the most resistant palates

765 Massachusetts Avenue (at Inman Street) / + 1 617 354 5433
lifealive.com / Open daily

True to writer stereotype, I sometimes subsist on black coffee and toast for days. Then a fierce craving for Life Alive hits me. Some serious sorcery goes on within the walls of this crunchy quick-serve spot. The wizardly chefs combine the world's healthiest ingredients to create unbelievably satisfying treats. The Goddess Bowl, for instance – kale, broccoli, avocado, almonds and brown rice in a ginger dressing – has the power to transform a fast-food junkie into a health nut with one forkful. As well as tasty food options, this healthy little haven also does delicious smoothies and fresh-pressed juices.

MR. BARTLEY'S GOURMET BURGERS

A Harvard Square emporium since 1960

1246 Massachusetts Avenue (at Plympton Street) / +1 617 354 6559
mrbartley.com / Closed Sunday

Like most fathers, mine is wary when it comes to "The Others", his not-so-endearing term for his children's beaus. But after one contender took him here, we discovered the way to his heart was as failsafe as it was clichéd: through his stomach. The walls are plastered in signage about celebrity regulars of the past and whether or not they were good tippers, providing perfect conversation pieces as you devour your burger, made in one of 36 configurations. Choice picks are The Big Papi (slathered in cheddar cheese and barbecue sauce) and The Beyoncé (Cajun-style with bacon and jalapeño), and don't forget a frappé — I recommend The Elvis (chocolate with Reese's and bananas "all shook up"), which is perhaps more famous around here than the King himself.

SOFRA BAKERY

Pocket-sized Middle Eastern pastry shop worth the trek

1 Belmont Street (at Holworthy Street) / +1 617 661 3161
sofrabakery.com / Open daily

Sofra is not on the way to Harvard Square, but Harvard Square is on the way to Sofra, the true hotspot center of Cambridge. Though it's a bit out of the way, don't even think about grabbing a mid-day bite elsewhere, tempted though you may be. Rarely is a bakery a destination in and of itself, but this one attracts foodies from far and wide, seeking novel recreations of sweet and savory Middle Eastern bites. The aroma of the tangy lamb shawarma with pickled turnips makes it difficult to stick to only stocking up on chocolate earthquake cookies, so save room for both.

THE TANNERY

Apparel for volatile weather

39 Brattle Street (between Church and Brattle Square)
+1 617 491 1811 / thetannery.com / Open daily

Boston's weather is so fickle that it's possible to experience all
four seasons in one day. Which means it's no easy feat to be practical
and stylish at once. In fact, it's a challenge not to look idiotic at times:
I've tied plastic bags over my shoes when a sudden downpour struck,
and Macgyvered a hand muff out of a T-shirt when the temperature
took a drastic dive. If you're suddenly tempted to do the same, head
straight to The Tannery, an upscale shop that boasts an expansive
collection of outerwear and athletic apparel. One word of caution:
your purchase might alter your stance on the forecast, rendering
you giddy during rainy days and snowstorms.

allston

brookline, jamaica plain

These three very different neighborhoods comprise what I like to call Boston's up and comers. Allston was once referred to as "student village" and was a tad dingy; today, the array of Harvard MBAs testing the start-up waters and budding musicians from Berklee make it a hipster's paradise. Neighboring Brookline, on the other hand, was once named the third snobbiest small city in America for good reason. It's home to the country's oldest private sporting club and is the birthplace of John F. Kennedy. Though it may be achingly uppercrust, the shops and restaurants are worth the splurge. Jamaica Plain - "JP" to the locals — is one of the first streetcar suburbs in America and remains one of Boston's most diverse and dynamic neighborhoods, despite growing more upscale as yuppie couples move in and demand dining and shopping options that meet their standards. Some central Boston residents believe there's no reason to leave the heart of the city, but the wisest of us know that these outlying areas offer many go-to destinations that are not to be missed.

1 Busy Bee Restaurant
2 Clear Flour Bread
3 Coolidge Corner Theater
4 Lone Star and Deep Ellum
5 Mint Julep

6 Oishii Sushi Bar
7 Salmagundi
8 Ten Tables
9 Tres Gatos
10 Zaftig's Delicatessen

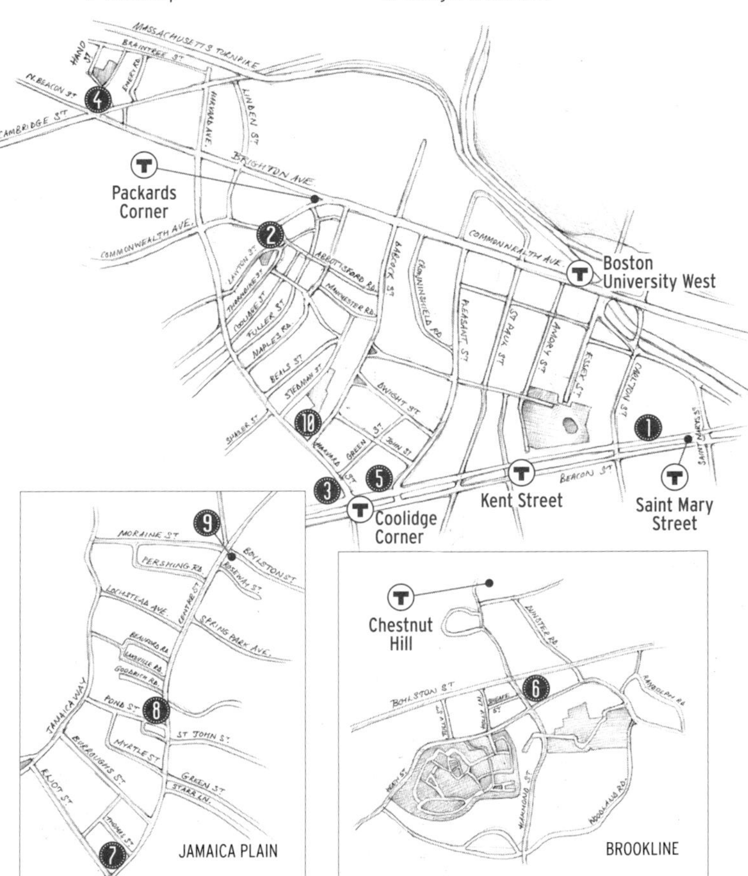

BUSY BEE RESTAURANT

Modest family-owned time capsule from 1967

1046 Beacon Street (between Carlton and St Marys)
+1 617 566 8733 / no website / Closed Sunday

When I mentioned this project to my friends, they were desperate for me to include Busy Bee Restaurant. With its retro décor and turquoise vinyl banquettes, it's our favorite neighborhood diner. They even proffered writing suggestions while recalling stories from previous visits: "It's the place that questions your character when you ask for light cream cheese," Susan offered (her request here elicited an eyebrow cock of epic proportions). "It's where you'll sit down with a big group and order 10 entrees, sides, juice and coffee for everyone, and have a tab that comes out to like, $23 total," Caleb added. He wasn't exaggerating: a plate heaping with eggs, toast and hash browns is $2.95. For folks who need not a single frill, this is it.

CLEAR FLOUR BREAD

Tiny family-owned neighborhood bakery

178 Thorndike Street (at Lawton Street) / +1 617 739 0060
clearflourbread.com / Open daily

In the age of gluten-free everything, I sometimes feel like I'm the only person who indulges in carbs anymore. Still, I'll fearlessly shout it from the rooftops: BREAD ROCKS. When I go to Clear Flour Bread, a 2015 semi-finalist for the James Beard Oustanding Baker Award, I always find my people, lined up on this quiet residential street well before the doors open, lured by the wafting aromas of authentic, freshly baked Italian, French and German bread. Some of Boston's top restaurants stock their bread baskets here — but the early-rising locals are likely after the luscious Gruyère and raspberry croissants, the stars of Clear Flour's international pastry selection.

COOLIDGE CORNER THEATER

Independent films as they were meant to be seen

290 Harvard Street (at Green Street) / +1 617 734 2501
coolidge.org / Open daily

When I walk into this non-profit independent cinema, I'm transported to a time when movies were glamorous affairs and people would dress to the nines to go to the pictures. The last giant silver screen in Boston, the theater was originally a Universalist church, but became a movie house in 1933, calling itself "a meeting place for the community, bringing culture and relief from care within the reach of all." A perfect marriage of art deco décor and modern amenities, Coolidge Corner Theater retains all its original charm and also serves adult beverages. The history of the building seems all too apropos, as it remains a place of worship – only now, to the art of film.

LONE STAR AND DEEP ELLUM

Neighboring hipster hangouts offering Allston's best grub

477 & 479 Cambridge Street (between North Beacon and Hano)
+1 617 782 8226 / lonestar-boston.com / Open daily
+1 617 787 2337 / deepellum-boston.com / Open daily

"We don't like labels here," quips our bartender when I wonder out loud why there's no sign outside besides, well... a lone star. Lone Star is the new addition to notorious hipster refuge Deep Ellum, so the nonconformist attitude doesn't surprise me. Side-by-side, these funky urban hideouts connect through the middle, making for a full night out – and a full stomach. While Deep Ellum is my go-to for craft beer and late-night nosh (three words: truffled gorgonzola fries), Lone Star is all about Mexican street food, mezcals and margaritas. With so many options, overindulging is inevitable. Still, it's impossible not to feel sexy in the dark, minimalist atmosphere, even when you're two tacos and a burger deep.

MINT JULEP

Changing the face of Boston's demure fashion

1302 Beacon Street (between Pleasant and Harvard)
+1 617 232 3600 / shopmintjulep.com / Open daily

I once offended a sizable chunk of Boston's female population when I called the fashion scene "pretty dismal, unless you consider Patagonias and Uggs très chic" in an interview. I'll take this as an opportunity to defend myself. Yes, we may err on the side of comfort when getting dressed for the day, but any lack of effort we display in daylight, we compensate for when the sun goes down. To be fair, our fervent endeavors don't always yield classy results. But Mint Julep can get us there. You'll recognize some designers you love from Newbury Street's Intermix, like Baily44 and BB Dakota, but you won't recognize the pieces — the buyers here have a knack for stocking the garments that aren't found in big name stores, ensuring you'll be uniquely en vogue.

OISHII SUSHI BAR

A secluded shrine to the art of sushi

612 Hammond Street (between Boylston and Heath)
+1 617 277 7888 / oishiiboston.com / Closed Monday

When my parents would visit me in college, their trips were dedicated to gourmandizing which meant I'd get a vacation from the dining hall. Weeks in advance, I'd begin highlighting my *Zagat* guide and posting restaurant reviews onto a bulletin board. When on one trip I suggested Oishii Sushi Bar, my dad was visibly perturbed by the hour long cab ride, and then when we arrived, the jam-packed, cramped quarters didn't help. But he was beaming in no time, because I'd uncovered Boston's best-kept sushi secret. With two new sister restaurants, this place is no longer under wraps, but it still reigns legendary – and for good reason. The innovative specialty maki menu is not to be missed: be sure to order the sudachi and seared hamachi maki, which comes with a sweet miso sauce.

SALMAGUNDI

Boston's top hat shop

765 Centre Street (between Thomas and Eliot)
+1 617 522 5047 / salmagundiboston.com / Open daily

I've a tendency to do terrible things to my hair when the dark depths of winter render me totally (albeit briefly) psychotic. Salmagundi is my saving grace. Even if you're not a hat person, I swear you'll leave here with a spring in your step and a teensy work of art perched atop your head. Perhaps it's the staff. Owner Jessen is so passionate about his craft that his enthusiasm is bound to rub off on you. Or perhaps it's the free Champagne bestowed upon those who walk in the door. Most likely, though, it's simply the huge selection of one-of-a-kind vintage and contemporary hats, from fedoras to fascinators, berets to bowlers, each of which has a storied history.

TEN TABLES

A small restaurant with big flavors

597 Centre Street (between Pond and Goodrich)
+1 617 524 8810 / tentables.net / Open daily

As the name suggests, Ten Tables is an eatery that's very modest in size, but titanic in reputation. With pasta and sausage handmade on the premises, this intimate neighborhood bistro draws a full crowd every evening. They offer a new dish nightly, but most go for the justly renowned four-course chef's tasting menu (vegetarian and vegan tasting menus offered, 24 hours advance notice needed for the vegan menu) that comes with four beverage pairings, and you'd be wise to do the same. If you'd rather sail your own ship, the all-natural burgers are incredibly juicy, but my pick is the creative short rib-stuffed burger with black truffle farmhouse cheddar and garlic aioli. You'll have to roll home afterward, but you won't be sorry.

TRES GATOS

Tapas, wine, books and music

470 Centre Street (between Roseway and Boylston)
+1 617 477 4851 / tresgatosjp.com / Open daily

I didn't think I was hip enough for the multi-faceted coolness of this all-in-one tapas restaurant, wine bar, bookshop and record store. Then I decided that even if I'd be the least cool person there, I wanted in. I'm so glad I went because, friends, it is amazing. This isn't a restaurant that sells books and music or vice versa; each aspect stands on its own merit. The tiny shop in the back has a small but superb selection, and the intimate restaurant is excellent. I'm a big fan of the patatas bravas and tortilla Española, but there are killer seasonal offerings as well. Wash it all down with a Jalapeño Business (smoked jalapeño tequila, grapefruit, lime and cilantro) and you'll be set.

ZAFTIG'S DELICATESSEN

Prepare to unleash your inner glutton

355 Harvard Street (between Babcock and Stedman)
+1 617 975 0075 / zaftigs.com / Open daily

While worshipping a melty mountain of banana-stuffed French
toast at this Jewish deli, I was informed that the Yiddish word zaftig
describes a woman with a full, round figure. I stopped chewing for
a split second, contemplated my destiny, decided to throw caution
to the wind and continued shoveling my meal down my gullet. The
portions here are outrageously ample, as is the menu of over 200
items, and they give you complimentary bagel chips and herb cream
cheese to start. The home-style chicken noodle soup is good enough
to make you crave a nasty cold, and even the most skeptical Jewish
mothers will kvell over the corned beef.

walk this way

The best spots to stroll

I don't mean to toot my own horn, but I have to say, I am a top-notch pedestrian. This will sound crazy – and believe me, I've received plenty of unsolicited psychoanalyses on the matter – but I have never driven a car, and I rarely take the subway. Luckily, Boston is small enough and safe enough that I can walk pretty much everywhere, and I always aim for the most scenic route possible.

My absolute favorite place to meander is **Commonwealth Avenue Mall**. The spine of Boston's elegant Back Bay and the largest Victorian neighborhood in the nation, these nine blocks of sheer magnificence feature spectacular brownstone homes in a grand, tree-lined allée that always looks stunning, but particularly so in winter, when tiny white lights illuminate each branch, forming a sparkling overhead arch.

Boston Public Garden is so spectacular it seems almost ostentatious. At every bend there's an explosion of vibrant flowers and the sweet serenade of an aspiring musician. Picturesque doesn't even begin to describe a place where one can spot swan families (yes, people: baby swans) nuzzling beneath colossal weeping willows.

In the summer, you can find me on the **South Boston Waterfront** – I'll be the one dreamily watching the auburn sun as it darts between skyscrapers and makes its dramatic exit for the night. As if its purpose is purely decorative, the water mirrors the sun setting over the city skyline as sailboats glide upon it.

Instagram aficionados, be sure to check out Beacon Hill's **Acorn Street**. It's only one block long but is reputed to be the most photographed street in the country, so it's safe to say that it's probably the most charming cobblestone road of all time. From here, transport yourself back to the 1800s as you explore **Louisburg Square**, an exclusive neighborhood that hasn't been touched in centuries.

And of course, for the American history buff, the renowned **Freedom Trail** is a 2.5-mile stretch marked by a red brick path that will take you past 16 significant locations, including graveyards, churches and the Paul Revere House. None of the sights are what you would call hidden gems, as each is easy to find and clearly marked, but still, the trail is not to be missed.

ACORN STREET
Between Mount Vernon and Chestnut

BOSTON PUBLIC GARDEN
Between Beacon and Boylston, +1 617 635 4505
cityofboston.gov/parks/emerald/Public_Garden.asp
open daily

COMMONWEALTH AVENUE MALL
Commonwealth Avenue (between Kenmore and Arlington), +1 617 634 4500, cityofboston.gov/Parks/emerald/Comm_Mall.asp, open daily

FREEDOM TRAIL
From Boston Common to U.S.S. Constitution
+1 617 357 8300, freedomtrail.org, open daily

LOUISBURG SQUARE
Between Pinckney and Mount Vernon

SOUTH BOSTON WATERFRONT
Along Boston Harbor, bostonsnewwaterfront.com
open daily